SUDDENLY RICH

SUDDENLY RICH

JERRY LeBLANC &
RENA DICTOR LeBLANC

Prentice-Hall, Inc., Englewood Cliffs, New Jersey

For Mia, Marisa, Jerry, Monique, and Norman
who enriched our lives.

Suddenly Rich by Jerry LeBlanc and Rena Dictor LeBlanc

Copyright © 1978 by Jerry LeBlanc and Rena Dictor LeBlanc

Printed in the United States of America
Prentice-Hall International, Inc., London/Prentice-Hall of Australia,
Pty.Ltd., Sydney/Prentice-Hall of Canada, Ltd., Toronto/Prentice-Hall of
India Private Ltd., New Delhi/Prentice-Hall of Japan, Inc., Tokyo/Prentice-
Hall of Southeast Asia Pte.Ltd., Singapore/ Whitehall Books Limited, Wel-
lington, New Zealand
10 9 8 7 6 5 4 3 2 1

Library of Congress Cataloging in Publication Data
LeBlanc, Jerry.
  Suddenly rich.

  1. Millionaires—United States—Biography.
2. Wealth—United States. I. LeBlanc, Rena Dictor,
                            joint author. II. Title.
HG172.A2L4   332'.092'2[B]   78-3491
ISBN 0-13-875609-0

Acknowledgments

The authors wish to acknowledge and extend thanks for the cooperation and assistance given to them by most of the major characters in this book. Real names are used in all but those few cases where identities were concealed to protect privacy. We also wish to thank for their help, the lottery commissions of several states, especially Illinois, Maryland, New Jersey, New York and Ohio. But our debt is greatest to the people who shared their experiences and insights with us, including behavioral scientists at universities from coast to coast. A special thanks goes to Dr. Charles William Wahl and Dr. Arnold L. Gilberg, psychoanalysts who offered many incisive comments on the problems of sudden wealth. We also thank United Artists Television, Inc., for permission to quote from the 1948 Warner Brothers' film, *The Treasure of Sierra Madre*.

Contents

...the race is not to the swift, nor the battle to the strong, neither yet bread to the wise, nor yet riches to men of understanding, nor yet favour to men of skill; but time and chance happeneth to them all.

—Ecclesiastes 9:11

Introduction

"If I only had a million dollars. . . ."
It's a common daydream, one that most people toy with at some point in their lives. But beyond its appeal as a fantasy game, responses to the question "What would you do if you had a million dollars?" carry enough significance that psychoanalysts routinely ask it in preparing the workup of a new patient's case history. Those responses reveal much about a person's mind.

In this book we tell the true stories of ordinary men and women from all walks of life, from all parts of the country, who *did* suddenly become rich—through a lottery, an inheritance, a marriage, a lucky break, or some other unexpected source. What happened to these people when a fortune suddenly came their way? Did it solve all their problems? Did they carry out their fantasies, fulfill all their dreams?

Whatever else sudden wealth brought about, it almost invariably resulted in a major upheaval in all their lives, producing emotions ranging from exhilaration to despair, and experiences, good or ill, that would otherwise never have occurred. One young woman used her money to pursue a dream of adventure up the Amazon. Another returned rich to the hometown where she'd been poor. A black ghetto-dweller packed up and moved to a mansion. One man took his family and hid like a fugitive, fearing kidnap. To one woman a million dollars simply meant she could fill up her freezer with steaks. Some foolishly squandered their money, while others were admirably cautious.

Curiosity about the rich seems to be a natural part of life in America, possibly because so many people nourish the conviction that someday, somehow, they'll be rich themselves. The struggle to attain greater wealth than we have occupies us daily as we pursue what sociologists call "upward mobility": the big promotion and raise, the luxury car, the lavish home in a nicer neighborhood—in short, the good life that it is generally assumed money can buy.

So much is this historic urge part of the American dream that despite the recent revolution in so many of our other attitudes and institutions, this one has survived reasonably intact. From the time that immigrants flocked to this nation in the belief that it was the Land of Opportunity (whether or not they believed the streets were "paved with gold"), the pursuit of wealth has been and continues to be deemed worthy of our most strenuous effort, whatever the odds of success.

"For an American," wrote the early sociological observer Alexis de Tocqueville in his 1830 classic *Democracy in America*, "the whole of life is treated like a game of chance, a time of revolution, or the day of a battle." And he spoke of "that intoxication which goes with sudden access to fortune," an intoxication available as nowhere else to the happy citizens of the New World. "The universal movement prevailing in the United States," de Tocqueville wrote, "the frequent reversals of fortune and the unexpected shifts in public and private wealth all unite to keep the mind in a sort of feverish agitation which wonderfully disposes it toward every type of exertion and keeps it, so to say, above the common level of humanity."

Put aside any doubts you may have as to whether this "feverish agitation" still exists. When, in September 1976, the State of New York resumed its million-dollar lottery after a year's suspension and sold nearly 20 million tickets the very first week, newspaper headlines followed a common theme: "NEW YORK," they cried, "HAS LOTTERY FEVER."

Fever, yes, but not madness. In *The Collected Papers of Otto Fenichel* (W. W. Norton & Co., 1954) the noted psychiatrist asked, "Is there an instinctual drive to amass wealth?" His answer: "There appears to be no possible doubt about this. We meet this drive every day in widely varying degrees in different people . . . indeed, a person in whom it is completely lacking will in our society be considered abnormal."

As we pursue our own individual drives toward riches, few of us are destined to reach the magic mark of a million dollars. Those who do make it—and the number of millionaires in America has soared in the last thirty years from 13,000 to well over 200,000—owe the credit as much to inflation as to accomplishment. Still, a powerful mystique surrounds those of us who have a million, and we always want to know more about that select club most of us dream of joining someday.

Our own particular curiosity about what millionaires are like had its beginning one Sunday afternoon a few years ago, when a wealthy friend of ours who had been poor as a child and was still much impressed by money opened the front door to his deluxe ranch house in Palm Springs, gestured inward with pride, and confided, rather solemnly, "In this room, there's a hundred million dollars."

The room—deep carpets, upholstery, a show of glass and paneling—was clearly upper middle class except for two card tables, each seating four aging men who were busy with a game of bridge. There was no pile of money in sight, and it was difficult to imagine all that cash stuffed in the unbulging pockets of these very ordinary-looking gentlemen. Their bank accounts, assets, or "net worth," as the phrase goes, may well have exceeded a $100 million because their names, when introductions were made, were vaguely familiar as film producers, industrialists, and the like. But to a stranger, hardly did there appear to be such a fortune in the room—only a group of perfectly ordinary and unremarkable-looking people passing a quiet Sunday afternoon in a perfectly ordinary and unremarkable way.

Rich people, you see, are not always readily identifiable as such. In fact, thinking now about millionaires of our acquaintance—including a flamboyant Texas heiress, an inventor, a rocket scientist, a sports entrepreneur, a fast food magnate, several celebrities from assorted fields, an unemployed king, and at least one successful thief—not one of them looks particularly rich, or acts rich, either. These millionaires have attained their wealth gradually, as a child reaches adulthood, and have grown accustomed to it. To them, being rich is nothing *special*, and thus calls for no special behavior.

Consider by contrast Paul F. McNabb, a thirty-year-old baker from Baltimore who won Maryland's first million-dollar state lottery. Hearing the news, McNabb leaped to his feet, grabbed the first woman within reach, whirled her in a victory dance, let out a rebel yell, and moments later, fainted dead away. Reviving quickly, he waved his prize money check and, grinning from ear to ear, began reciting joyously to one and all how he was going to spend his fortune: "I'm movin' West—by way of Tokyo, Rome, Paris, and the world. Yahoo!"

His delightful non-nonchalance encouraged us to proceed in a direction in which we were already moving: to write a book about what an abundance of money does to people, not a book about millionaires of long standing but rather about people like Mr. McNabb, people who had recently been (at least relatively) poor and who had suddenly become rich, people who had suddenly been plunged, by fate or otherwise, into a new world where their lifelong attitudes toward hard work and thrift could be thrown out the window. All the dreams these men and women had harbored for years, all the things they would have done if only they had the money, now could be fulfilled. Or could they?

To answer that and many other questions, we began our research, interviewing dozens of people from all parts of the country who had, in one way or another, attained sudden wealth. The experiences of people at this turning point in their lives, the conflict of joy and fear they were thrown into, posed other questions which we took to experts in the behavioral sciences for their comments.

We approached our subject as journalists, that is, as observers and reporters, rather than as psychologists or sociologists. But in telling faithfully what we saw and heard of these peoples' lives, we are dealing in facts which provide considerable insight into human behavior. We believe that the case histories reported here form not merely an anthology of parallel experiences, but a composite view of that category of events which can lift people abruptly out of their accustomed class, economic level, and lifestyle, and open doors that before were only remotely known to exist. Their behavior makes a significant comment on the attitudes toward money and other values by which all of us dream and live.

Let's return now to the matter of normality, not in terms of our drive for wealth but rather in terms of our attitudes toward the wealthy. It seems "normal" to display an ambivalent feeling about people who are rich. On the one hand we admire, envy, imitate, and emulate them. We are curious about, even fascinated by them. We imagine them to be different from ordinary people and hold them in awe. But our admiration is not unmixed with resentment. We like to laugh at things that rich eccentrics do, to scorn their wasteful indulgences, and we regard their power and privileges with suspicion.

There are familiar biblical admonitions about rich men,

and literature for centuries has disparaged them. Thoreau once said, "Absolutely speaking, the more money, the less virtue."

Steinbeck once complained to a friend about the incursion of free-spending tourists and wealthy retirees into his beloved Monterey: "I don't mind people, you know that, but these are rich people."

It's even in our language, the tendency to couple the word "rich" with "idle" or "filthy."

Our ill feelings toward the rich were clearly pointed out in one simple but elegant experiment conducted recently by a Florida State University social scientist, Dr. Russell Clark. He parked two different vehicles in a New York suburban shopping center night after night, one a new gold Cadillac, presumably a wealthy man's, and the other an older, medium-priced Ford. Each vehicle was parked with lights burning and windows down. Passers-by turned off the Ford's lights 82 percent of the time, while the Cadillac's lights were turned off only 39 percent of the time. "The experiment had to be called off," commented Dr. Clark, "because the man who owned the Cadillac was getting fed up with having a burned-out battery every morning."

Similarly, in West Germany, behaviorists recently arranged for a working-class man to return from vacation driving a status-symbol gold Cadillac worth over $20,000, twice what the man earned in a year. When he offered no explanation for the vehicle, his neighbors and co-workers began avoiding him and treating him with great suspicion. Meanwhile, hotel doormen began showing him deference, and he found he could always leave the Cadillac in "No Parking" zones without being ticketed.

This love-hate ambivalance toward the rich is a feeling of which the rich themselves are well aware. One wealthy man gave the view from his side of the class barrier to psychoanalyst Charles William Wahl: "I have all my life been used to people viewing me as a resource, a symbol, rather than a person. I early learned to pick up the greed and resentment in their eyes. This always had a great deal to do with my cynical mistrust of everyone."

At the very heart of the conflict between the rich and poor emerges the issue of luck, which to many have-nots is the only acceptable reason why the rich are rich and the poor are poor. Yet even our attitude toward luck is curious, because in a sense we believe that good luck is earned. When fortune smiles on someone, we ask, "What did he do to deserve such good luck?"

When William M. Fisher, a retired bachelor from Laurel, Maryland, won a million dollars in a lottery and boasted of a steady streak of good luck, his sister explained, "He's a good-hearted man; that's why he wins."

A number of big lottery winners attributed their good luck to God, who, we had heard, did not encourage gambling. "There must be something shining down on me," explained million-dollar winner John Sartoretti of New York in a typical victory statement. "I'm Catholic and I haven't been going to church lately, but I'm going to start now."

Belief in the intervention of deity in our games of chance is often expressed by lottery winners. Apparently, becoming rich is considered an Act of God singling out the worthiest of individuals for one of His highest blessings on earth. If God doesn't do it then it's Luck or Fate. It's generally conceded that an unseen hand—not a blind and random thing—selects those who will be elevated from the lower to the monied class.

What is required of those of us who would embark on the road to riches? Bankers sometimes marry chorus girls, certainly, but their women frequently offer outstanding charms in return. Still, theoretically, in this land of few rigid social barriers, any woman can meet and marry a millionaire.

As for unexpected inheritances, we are a mobile, transient people and many of us lose track of even our closest relatives and friends, so the situation of a surprise inheritance is neither unique nor now even rare, though it does require a long-lost relative. Waitresses and an occasional good Samaritan also fall heir to large bequests, but as a rule these involve at least a minimal display of companionship or kindness.

Treasure hunters and gamblers require a spirit of adventure that is not universal, and often a measure of skill, too. Moreover, even today, the Horatio Alger story is dominated by the theme that the way to wealth is through long years of hard work, with no assurance of ultimate success.

It is the lottery, finally, that stands out today as the purest source of instant riches; that's why this book pays more attention to lottery prize winners than to any other achiever of windfall wealth. Who needs a brilliant idea, a special talent, or a rich uncle? All are superseded by the perfect democracy of the lottery, in which the only qualifications are eighteen years of life (if that) and the price of a ticket. It's surely the way to wealth best suited to this age of instant gratification. Anybody who plays can win, and sometimes you don't even have to play. One New Jersey hardware dealer who sold lottery tickets as a sideline was obliged by the rules to pay for two dozen unsold tickets. After grumbling and paying, he discovered one of the tickets was worth $50,000. And more than once, gift tickets have enriched the receiver far beyond the giver's own means.

The enthusiasm of people about the prospect of instant riches through the new state lotteries, where "millionaires" are created regularly by chance and the state government, can be witnessed weekly as crowds form lines to buy tickets the minute they go on sale. Some outlets are sold out in the first few hours. Millions are playing the game.

Why do they do it? To escape the rat race of struggling with bills, mortgage and car payments, college tuition, and saving for retirement, and they believe that just one big windfall will do it. They have seen luck help others to escape the demeaning impotence of insufficient funds, and they too want to escape. Fifty cents or a dollar or two a week lets them try, and sustains a dream more tangible than any other they may have. Buying hope on the installment plan, they wait for the day when the American Dream is not pie in the sky in the great by-and-by, but, if they want it, filet mignon on the dinner table seven nights a week.

Is there something new developing in the American spirit, something that makes people refugees from the traditional belief in the rewards of hard work and thrift?

In Liberty Farms, Indiana, a 44-year-old salesman quit his job and began driving around thirteen states from Illinois eastward to the Atlantic where lotteries are held. "It's my profession now," he declared. "I'm going to play the lotteries until I hit it big."

In Pennsylvania, Tom Drake and his wife Philomena began selling all their possessions to raise $20,000, which they planned to "invest" in lottery tickets. "We want to win a thousand dollars a week for life," said Drake. "We'll risk everything for a chance at it."

More than one observer of the American scene has noted the danger of such all-or-nothing daring, which might become contagious if the Drakes or someone like them ever landed a million-dollar prize. But there may be danger as well even in fifty-cent betters winning that kind of sum week after week in state after state. Just what does it do to the millions of hard-working people when they see lotteries and twists of fate lifting others no better or worse than themselves out of the financial struggle, almost exempt from the human condition?

Whether or not we individually become rich, futurologists predict that we are all headed toward an age of greater leisure, and it's interesting to note that many of the suddenly rich who quit their jobs find it a problem to deal with an abundance of leisure time. Relieved of economic pressure, of bosses and time clocks, they are also deprived of a structure in their daily lives. That much freedom can be terrifying. The noted psychiatrist and social observer Franz Alexander has written, "It is paradoxical but nonetheless true that the nearer man comes to his goal, to make his life easy and abundant, the more he undermines the foundations of a meaningful existence. . . ."

Sudden wealth can pose many problems, and for most

of them people are completely unprepared. It can precipitate a major family crisis. It can sorely test people's images of themselves. It can threaten friendships, put a strain on sexual relations, and even give rise to a deep sense of guilt. Uncomfortable among the upper class if they move to better neighborhoods, the suddenly rich may question the value of the "upward mobility" to which they may have devoted much of their lives. Class consciousness still rules our attitudes to a great extent, and nothing in the experience of becoming suddenly rich ensures that these "lucky" few will not spend the balance of their lives with a terrible sense of dislocation, of being "out of place."

But none of these problems are likely to dissuade people from the desire, and the attempt, to become rich. While psychologists theorize that money fantasies, like sexual fantasies, seldom turn out as well in real life as in the dream, the experiences of the suddenly rich manifest a joy, an excitement, and for some a sense of security never known before, all of which argue convincingly that rich, whatever the pitfalls, is decidedly better. Dr. Wahl, the psychoanalyst, has stated, "The rich, being a member of a small minority group, display many of the apparent identification difficulties (such as suspicion of outsiders, loneliness, and isolation) that are generally characteristics of any minority group." But it's a minority group that everybody wants to join.

"If there is such a thing as a history of human attitudes," Dr. Alexander said in his *History of the Western Mind in Transition* (Random House, 1960), "it consists of the sum total of the ever-changing subjective experiences of those who participate in it." Such case history reports, Alexander added, can constitute "one of the most valuable types of information about characteristic emotional attitudes of a period." A man who studied under Alexander, Dr. Arnold Gilberg, whose psychiatric practice gives him broad experience with the emotional problems of the wealthy, has contributed some insightful observations to this book. We are greatful also for the comments of Dr. Wahl, whose paper, "Psychoanalysis of the Rich, the Famous and the Influential," contains the comment, "It was surprising to note on perusal of the literature that this subject has seemingly never been studied."

The field remains open. Although much has been said and written in popular books and the media about individual wealthy men, and in textbooks about wealth in society, this book is the first to treat as a class what might be termed the "windfall hero"—a unique group of people involved in a challenging and much-envied social and economic adventure. If this book is judged meaningful, it won't be entirely because of what we say about these suddenly rich or what they say about themselves, but also largely from what you, the reader, are able to discover about your own attitudes toward wealth, sudden or otherwise.

1. The Lotteries

When they turned off the gas and the telephone in Judy Lutes's small Chicago apartment, it seemed to her that her life had hit rock bottom. How could she explain to her little son that his father had gone away and wouldn't be coming back, that there was no money left to pay the bills? Trying to make the best of it, she played games with the child to help them both forget how cold it was. Then they went to bed early, bundled in layers of clothing to keep warm.

Cuddling together with the child until he dropped off to sleep, she lay in the darkness with her eyes open, thinking, "If only I had enough money, at least enough to pay the bills." And she told herself, not really believing it but trying to anesthetize the pain of poverty, "Some day I'll have money."

A pleasant-looking young woman with lively blue eyes and a warm, tilted smile, she was used to toughening herself when things went wrong, and she'd developed a stubborn streak, a fierce independence that made her refuse the help friends offered in times like this.

Poverty was nothing new to Mrs. Lutes. She had been dirt poor as a child in Alabama where she lived with three sisters, three brothers, and their parents in a four-room, square wood frame house. A fireplace provided the only heat and the kids had to pile together in the same bed in the winter to keep warm. Her father worked off and on at a lumber mill and sometimes as a truck driver. Her mother made clothes for the children out of flour sacks. The only luxury she could remember was when the family bought an old piano and she started taking lessons, but it lasted merely six months because the family could no longer afford the lessons at fifty cents a week. Then, when she was twelve, her parents divorced and her mother went to work operating a punch press in a factory.

Without finishing high school, Judy had married as a teenager and moved to Chicago, where her son was born. He was only two years old when Judy herself was divorced, and the hard times followed. Now she had to take charge of things herself, get a job, and try to stretch out the money she could earn to support herself and the boy. It wouldn't be easy, but she was determined to stand on her own two feet.

Her days were long. Mrs. Lutes found a job as a clerk in a lawyer's office in the Loop. It meant getting up at five-thirty each morning, taking her boy to nursery school or to a baby-sitter, and traveling across town to the office. When her full-time job was over for the week, she worked tending bar in a tavern Fridays and Saturdays from eight o'clock until three the next morning, and on Sunday afternoons she cleaned people's houses.

In time, she worked her way up to legal secretary in the same office where she'd started and reached the point where she could afford the rent on a two-bedroom home in the middle-class suburb of Melrose Park. She devoted herself fully to her son, to her job, and to taking care of the home. There wasn't much time or money for anything else.

One cold, wintry day she was doing her regular grocery shopping at the Jewel Market in a block of stores near her home. She chose the items she needed carefully, passing up the steaks she loved and settling for more economical foods, keeping a watch out for special sale prices. At the checkstand, her practicality wavered a moment. Impulsively, she told the cashier, "And give me a lottery ticket."

It turned out to be the best one-dollar purchase she ever made. Two months later the Illinois State Lottery Commission randomly picked the five-digit number on the ticket she held. Mrs. Judy Lutes became a millionaire.

In 1976 an estimated 1.5 billion lottery tickets were sold in the thirteen states from Illinois to the eastern seaboard where official state lotteries were then operated. Several other states in the Midwest and West are preparing to spread the game from coast to coast, and experts predict that it's only a matter of time before a majority of the states, probably excluding the Deep South Bible Belt, join in the action.

At least eight states offer million-dollar prizes, usually paid at the rate of $50,000 a year for twenty years. Since 1970, almost two hundred people from all walks of life have been plucked by chance from the common struggle and elevated to positions of wealth beyond all previous expectations. They became "instant millionaires." Hundreds of other people, with less flourish than that reserved for the magic million mark, walked off more quietly with substantial awards ranging from $10,000 to $200,000—small fortunes, perhaps, but more than enough to change a life.

A married secretary in Boston, a policeman in Peoria, an Indian in Ohio, a widow in New Jersey, a staff sergeant in the Air Force, a retiree in Seattle, a Pennsylvania steel mill worker, barmaids and clerks, truck drivers and factory workers have all joined the ranks of lottery millionaires, while countless people like them bet weekly and pray to be chosen too.

"We're selling dreams," proclaimed one state. And the people are buying. What they are buying is hope. It's their secret transaction with Fate on the only grounds where negotiations are open.

Judy Lutes, millionaire. Mrs. Judy Lutes, the Chicago divorcee who once had struggled to support herself and her son, sat behind her busy desk in her small, bright but windowless office in a law firm on the sixth floor of a tall Loop building. Tacked on the inside of her door was a 1975 certificate attesting that she had won a million dollars in the Illinois State Lottery. In her early thirties, an open-faced woman with an engaging manner, she had a kind of straightforward honesty about her. She wore no makeup, her short brown hair was in a no-nonsense style, her rounded figure was a shade fuller than stylish, her slacks and top perfectly ordinary, off-the-rack clothes, and her old shoes torn but comfortable. She smiled easily and shared an unforced camaraderie with her bosses and the other people in her office as she talked with us about her big lottery win:

"I kind of forgot about the lottery ticket after I bought it till one day in November. My son was home from school with a cold. I was at the laundromat because my dryer was broke. Suddenly he came charging into the laundromat not even wearing his jacket. He told me he'd seen on television that I was one of the lottery winners. I thought he was teasing me and I told him, 'I'll kill you for coming out with no coat when you're sick.' But he kept saying it was true.

"Then, at ten o'clock I heard them say it on the news, that I was one of the winners and was eligible for the million dollars. We had to wait. It wasn't until January they had the million-dollar drawing. Forty names had been drawn and all of us were asked to come down to a television studio where they would narrow the finalists down to ten and then pick a jackpot winner.

"I went down to the studio with my son, my sister, my

niece, her girlfriend, and my own best girlfriend. I was so nervous I took six tranquilizers before I left. We had to wait in this little room and it was so hot and I know I had this blank look on my face waiting for the results of the drawings.

"I was picked number seven and they moved us ten finalists out to sit with the studio audience. They had a video tape horse race, and when they showed it, the number of the horse that won would be the million-dollar winner. Everybody with me was standing up and screaming, rooting for the number seven horse when they showed them going around the track. My horse was ahead but I didn't even get up.

"I just sat there because I figured for sure my horse would get beat out at the wire, you know. I've never won anything before so it just didn't seem likely that I would win. But suddenly it was number seven leaving the others behind as it passed the finish line. The next thing I knew someone was calling my name and I have no idea how I made it to the stage. That's a total blank to me. I was sitting behind this row of people and I don't know if I went over them, around them, under them or what. Suddenly I was on stage and my friends and family were there with me.

"While everyone was congratulating me, I remembered my friend Gus. He's an old guy who's recuperating from a stroke and when I'd visit him and clean for him he kept telling me I was going to win, so I promised, 'When I win, I'll say Hi to you on TV.' So I asked the emcee right in the middle while he was talking to me, I said, 'Can I say something?' And I said into the microphone, 'Hey Gus, I did it!' That was the headline in the paper the next day, 'Hey Gus, She Did It.'

"Afterwards, I wanted to celebrate with a drink but I realized I didn't have any money. So I called my boss and his wife and asked if I could borrow some money, but he said he'd buy. Later I stopped at some friends', then I visited another friend who answers the phone in a pizzeria.

"When I got home I was grateful my phone isn't listed, so only a few people called that night. But the next day my son got so aggravated with the phone ringing and my family calling. The next week at work was unbelievable. The phones didn't stop ringing, and all these people we know were in and out of the office all the time. It was really wild.

"One of my bosses, who I've been with thirteen years, is really a crazy guy. He came crawling to my door on his hands and knees and said, 'Is it all right if I come in?' For a week and a half it was wild.

"I used to get phone bills, light bills, gas bills, from people that had ten children and wanted me to pay their bills. There was a letter from this guy in the penitentiary asking me to send him money. A lot of weirdos. My boss helped me put together a form letter saying, '... Of course I'd like to help everyone, but I can't. I have to choose an organization and do it through them. ...' So I did that.

"I had to wait a month before I got the first check from the lottery. I was nervous every day when I went to check the mailbox, but finally when I saw the letter I knew what it was, and I tore it open and just stared at it. It was for $50,000. It came on a weekend so I couldn't put it in the bank right away, so I hid it under the Marie Antoinette doll on the bureau in my room.

"On Monday I ran to the bank with it and everybody at the bank said 'Let me see, Judy, Let me see.'

"Then, the first thing, I took my son to the grocery store, and we really had fun. I told him, 'Get a cart. All the things that you want that we could never afford before, get 'em!'

"That was our big thrill. We must have got everything. I just went to the steak section and said, 'I'll take that one and that one and that one and that. ...' We spent $157, and for me and him that's a lot of money for a week's worth of groceries.

"And that's the only way winning a million changed my life is that I eat better. I drive the same 1974 Cougar I had before I won, and I'm going to drive it until the wheels fall off. I still just go around in jeans all the time. I'm not interested in clothes.

"Oh, I spent some money. I bought the house I'd been renting. That was a fantastic feeling. And me and my son went on a two-week trip to Hawaii, which was great, but we had to come back early because he wouldn't stay out of the pool long enough to keep the suntan lotion on and he got second degree burns on his shoulders. But I enjoyed the trip. I took a trip to Mexico one time and to Las Vegas another time, with women friends, but I wasn't impressed by those places.

"And my relatives. I bought an inexpensive house for my younger sister in Alabama and I had a lot of repairs done on my mother's house, got her some furniture, a color television and a new car. And I paid for a wedding, one of my nieces, and I got a bedroom set for two other nieces, things like that.

"I'm not going to spoil my son, though. I want my son to work for the things he wants. He'll appreciate it more and take care of the things he gets more. His friends kidded him about the money at first. They just expected he was going to get all these fantastic things. A reporter asked him what he wanted and he said a CB radio, but I never got him one. He doesn't need one.

"I'm a tough mother, but he's my pride and joy. I want him to grow up and be all right. I don't want him to grow up and have a cocky attitude. So I'm strict with him.

"One thing I want is to make sure my mother is taken care of. She's 62 and has quite a while left. I want to make sure she doesn't want for anything. My son can wait. He's young. My mother, she shouldn't have to wait, because she's my mother.

"Otherwise, I want my life to stay as normal as possible, especially for my son. So I still get up at five-thirty every morning and come to work by six-thirty. That way I beat the traffic.

"I'd never give up my job even though I have this lottery money now. I'd go nuts. I enjoy the people I work with. I even dread going on a two-week vacation. They'll have everything goofed up by the time I get back, and it will take me a month to get things straightened out.

"I like being single. I wouldn't have gotten married again, not before I won, and for damn sure I wouldn't get married now.

"Oh, I forgot. I started taking piano lessons again. I was taking piano when I was a kid—my God that was twenty years ago—and now I'm taking piano lessons again.

"I don't feel like a millionaire. Not when I go home from work and wash dishes every day. It's silly, but I don't have a dishwasher. My sister-in-law keeps telling me, 'Why don't you get someone in to do your house cleaning, your washing, your ironing?' but I tell her, 'I'll do it myself when I get around to it.' I don't want someone coming in doing *my* housework.

"I don't want to change my life. I still buy lottery tickets, but I don't want to win again, that's not it. What I buy them for is to make a collage for my house. I buy them and paste them on the wall."

"Buy this ticket. It could change your life," asserts the state of New York in advertisements to its citizens, and they do buy, believing throngs lining up for their lottery tickets, accepting the fact that this is their one chance in a million of transcending the dreary workaday life and rising into the leisure class. The odds are astronomical, but somebody's got to win. One chance in 25 million—the actual odds in New York—is better than no chance at all.

"The reason people buy these tickets is, simply, because it's a chance to win a large enough sum of money to change their lives," says Edward J. Powers of New Hampshire, former president of the National Association of State Lotteries. "There's really no other way they can do it."

When New Hampshire started its lottery in 1964, it was

nothing new. The Congress of the new nation as early as 1776
authorized a national lottery which lasted well into the
nineteenth century, and several of the foremost universities
in America owe their original endowments to lottery funds.
On a smaller scale, lotteries have been used to finance the
construction of many churches. No less a person than Thomas
Jefferson praised lotteries as a revenue measure where
"the tax is laid on the willing only."

Other countries, more than fifty of them throughout the
world, including Russia, Canada, West Germany, Denmark,
Spain, Mexico, and Portugal, have operated legal popular
lotteries for years, but their prizes do not compare with the
million-dollar bonanzas offered in the United States. Even
though some national lottery prizes worth up to $30 million
have been awarded in some foreign countries, the ticket-
selling process has always resulted in dozens or often hundreds of individuals owning a fraction of the winning ticket.
In America, when a ticket buyer pays his fifty cents or a dollar, he wants all of the big prize, not just a hundredth share.

"It's because of the astronomical top prize, that people
buy these tickets," says Priscilla Smith, vice-president of Scien-
tific Games Development Corporation in Atlanta, the firm
which designed the lotteries for a half dozen states. "They
want to change their lives. The hope is there; they know the
odds are slim, but they know they *can* win. It can happen. The
credibility is there. And it's also a cheap form of entertain-
ment."

For fifty cents or a dollar a week people nourish the
dream of telling off the boss, buying a yacht and sailing
around the world, moving into their dream house in a better
area, living a life of ease, or just easing the pressure of bills, of
insecurity, of discontent.

In the vast Union Station in Chicago there's a section of
counters where you can buy costume jewelry, magazines,
candy, cigarettes—and dreams. A young black man sits behind a glass cage in the train station, deeply immersed in a
copy of *Reader's Digest*. A green paper in the window of the

cubicle reads, "The Illinois State Lottery Certificate of
License as Lottery Sales Agent." Close by is another sign that
says "Playday" and lists ticket numbers that have won. There's
also a picture of a rainbow and a pot of gold, with the printing, "Illinois State Lottery. THE $1,000,000 BONANZA!"

The train station is said to be the second busiest lottery
sales location in Chicago. From this place of high ceilings,
marble-like floor, wooden benches, and people scurrying in
all directions, one would no more expect dreams to emerge
than butterflies. Yet every few minutes a man or woman steps
up to the counter and buys a ticket that might mean an early
retirement, a new home, college educations for the kids, a
new car, a European vacation. A ticket, and a dream.

Robert Lavely, a factory worker, waits for his change at
the window. He buys a couple of tickets a week. What does he
want? "If I won I'd move out of Galesburg, get away from it
all," he says. "I'd travel."

Jesse Taylor, a mailman, buys three tickets a week: "If I
won a million I'd pay off my bills, invest in the stock market,
buy a new car, and go on vacation in Hawaii."

Charles Dederici, a purchasing agent: "If I won a million
I'd take time off from work, go on a trip and see this beautiful
country."

Frank Miller, an accountant: "If I won I'd retire. I'd play
golf and just loaf."

And as for the dispenser of all these possibilities, the
young man selling tickets—who is also a regular purchaser—
looked up from his magazine and told his dream: "I'd like to
be an accountant."

Paul McNabb, 30 years old, lived in a rented, two-bedroom
house in Baltimore with his wife and two children. They had
no car since the last one broke down, didn't even have a
telephone, and McNabb never dared miss a day's work as a
doughnut baker lest the family budget crack under the strain.
Actually, it was night work. Every night the small, thin, hand-

some McNabb mixed 80 pounds of dough at the Dunkin'
Donut Shop in the Baltimore suburb called Reistertown. Cutting the dough into shape by hand, he took pride in the swift-
ness and precision of his work, deep-frying the doughnuts,
coating them with various frostings, and placing them by the
dozen on tall racks to be wheeled away.

He usually bought at least one lottery ticket a week,
more often two, stopping on his way to work or while shopping. On the week that Maryland launched its new, bigger-
than-ever, million-dollar prize, McNabb could only spare the
money for one ticket, which he got at the Thrifty Wise Store.

Like Judy Lutes and dozens of others, Paul McNabb hit
the jackpot. When he was selected the winner, as we reported
earlier, he leaped to his feet, let out a rebel yell, seized the first
woman he could reach, and danced her in a circle, then
fainted. Revived, he found himself not only suddenly rich,
but suddenly famous as well. As the first of that state's
million-dollar winners, he enjoyed celebrity status of the first
rank. Maryland printed tens of thousands of play-money
million-dollar bills that carried McNabb's picture, and distributed them everywhere to promote the lottery. Newspaper
reporters beat a path to his doughnut shop, where he kept on
working until his boss, to whom McNabb was grateful for past
kindnesses, could find a replacement. McNabb, who had
never before been in the public eye or been asked his opinion
about anything but doughnuts, now posed for the news
cameras and was interviewed on television, radio, and in the
press.

A simple, outgoing man unashamed of his small-town
origins in the hills of Virginia, he drawled in slangy English
about his plans for the million dollars. Asked if the money was
going to change him, he responded promptly and sincerely:
"Do you mean the class of person I am? If you mean the class
of person I am, the answer is no, I'm goin' to stay the same
honest, hard-workin', God-fearin' man I've always been."

But gradually his whole life began to turn around. With
the first of his twenty annual checks for $50,000, McNabb

wanted to indulge himself to the hilt. After years of frugality, he and his wife Winnie, a small, shy woman a year younger than he, went on a shopping spree to start things off, determined to blow the first check just by having fun. But it was a restrained spree. Their biggest purchases were a jeep and new furniture.

Paying a year's rent in advance, McNabb put the rest of his money in the bank. Then he fished and hunted until he'd filled his thirst for the great out-of-doors. If he got bored doing nothing, he'd go back and put in a few days work at the doughnut shop. Because of McNabb's celebrity status, the proprietor was always glad to see him come back; he'd put Paul to work in the storefront window where he was sure to attract crowds of passers-by. "When he comes back to work," said the boss, "we do more business than ever."

Gradually, McNabb became mistrustful of people and resentful of the publicity. He would still let people touch him for good luck if they asked, but he refused to sign his autograph on the phony million-dollar bills. He even stopped answering his "fan mail," fearful of what unscrupulous strangers might do with a copy of his handwriting.

One day the final straw came. People had often stopped his wife or children on the street to speak to them and ask questions, and he had always put up with that. But one day a television interviewer thrust a microphone at his younger daughter Monica, seven years old, and asked her how she felt about all the money and all the attention. She blurted out tearfully, "I wish daddy would give all the money back."

McNabb stopped appearing in public. He shut himself off so completely that he could be reached only by a complex routine of telegrams to an intermediary. The family began moving from state to state, Pennsylvania, North Carolina, Nevada. Once he was spotted gambling in Las Vegas—betting a dollar a throw. And then after a few years, the McNabbs settled quietly in a western state. Maryland had meanwhile created other millionaire celebrities and the whole furor had died down.

"I'm happy," he says now, without conviction, "because I know that no matter what happens, I'll always have a roof over my head. But it's really somethin' how drastic your life changes. I swore up and down I wasn't goin' to change, but I did." The biggest change, he admitted, is that he doesn't trust people as much as he used to. "It all come up too sudden. I wasn't ready for all of it. It was much easier when I was just a simple baker."

The process of elevating an ordinary citizen from the workaday ranks to the lofty status of financial comfort begins with the simple purchase of a lottery ticket, but it ends in a circus atmosphere designed by the lottery promoters to give maximum public exposure to the event.

Finalists for the million-dollar prize—sometimes as few as two dozen and sometimes more than a hundred—assemble in an auditorium, at a State Fair or in a television studio. (Several states televise their drawings regularly and the local ratings indicate they are watched by many more people than is the network news.) Whether the system for selecting winners depends on the outcome of a horse race or employs little plastic balls containing finalists' names, the "show" delivers celebrities, music, girls, balloons, and all the fanfare in a staging that resembles, not accidentally, a television game show. Bob Hope, Frank Sinatra, Telly Savalas, Yul Brynner, Dean Martin, Jerry Lewis, and countless other show business luminaries have participated in the drawings, which are calculated to wring from the finalists their last perspiring drop of emotion.

The resemblance of lottery drawings to giveaway shows is no accident, owing much (but by no means all) to the fact that some executives of the firm that designed most of the state lottery systems were once with a company that packaged game shows for televison. Unlike the network game shows contestants, however, who are pretested for the openness of their responses, coached to jump up and down to demonstrate excitement, and warned they must smile a lot and look happy, the lottery finalists for the most part have no aspirations to show business, and no preparation. Though lottery rules usually require them to be there, they often act as if they would rather be somewhere else, and notified of the outcome by telephone. Awkward moments occur time and time again when winners stand dumbfounded, or faint, or, at the urgings of masters of ceremonies or members of the press, give silly answers to sillier questions. One television reviewer who tuned in to a drawing was aghast at the "incredibly amateurish show" and was at a loss to explain, on aesthetic grounds, why it was on the public airways.

The hoopla surrounding the selection of lottery millionaires frequently means trouble for the winners, also, because they not only are unprepared for wealth, but are equally unprepared for the fame which results from media exposure. The big drawing not only gives one money, it makes one the man or woman of the hour, an instant celebrity, prey to all the public hounding that celebrities must endure. The major difference: other celebrities *seek* fame and usually have years of gradual adaptation to it. Not so the lottery winners, to whom it can be unwanted, annoying, even traumatic.

"The last time I was at Jones Beach it was to fish for bass," said actor Yul Brynner. "Today, I'm going to fish for a million dollars."

It was not the kind of joke that would make Don Rickles or Bob Hope fearful of Brynner moving in on their territory. But the lucky lottery ticket holders who had made it to the finals of the New York State Lottery's Million Dollar drawing, along with their friends and family who were Brynner's open-air, stadium audience, exploded in laughter from pent-up emotion.

The runner-up $20,000 winners had already been called, and now Brynner prepared to open the envelope and read the name of the million-dollar lottery winner. With another stab at humor he told the crowd, "I'll take the envelope with me and announce the winner at the Uris Theater where I'm performing tonight."

The bleachers of the Jones Beach Marine Theater were sparsely occupied, and what crowd there was clustered near the stage where Brynner, lottery officials, bandleader Guy Lombardo (who had helped pick earlier winners), and two decorative young women in orange gowns took part in the presentations. The wind set flags of many colors fluttering along the top edge of the stadium seats. Just beyond the stage, ocean waves lapped gently, and in the distance the beach was lined with people who had managed to escape the city on a Friday afternoon.

People squinted toward the stage in the bright sunlight, tension mounted, and a drum roll began. A dozen reporters and cameramen stood by, ready to pounce at the proper moment.

Brynner read off the first name, "Michael," and a squeal of excitement rose from one end of the bleachers. Masses of people stood up to get a better view. Brynner pronounced the last name, "Johnson," and the squeals faded amid a murmur of disappointment and loud groans from losers in the crowd. Others strained to catch a glimpse of the New York Lottery's newest millionaire. One almost expected a ray of sunlight, like some cosmic spotlight, to light the path for the momentous occasion. But instead, a young man in a dingy, torn T-shirt, jeans and tennis shoes, with long brown hair and a moustache, inched his way down the bleacher stairs.

As he slowly made his way up to the stage, looking lost, pale, and scared, the band played rousing choruses of "We're in the Money," "There'll Be a Hot Time in the Old Town Tonight," and other appropriate tunes. No sooner was Johnson on stage to collect the first of the thousand-dollar checks he'll receive each week for the rest of his life than reporters and cameramen engulfed him, brushing aside

Brynner. Johnson, looking rather like a trapped animal, responded in a barely audible voice to the questions hurled at him from all sides. There was a hush as he spoke.

"Guess I took a while to come down to the stage," he said vaguely. "I didn't know what I was supposed to do."

With cameras aiming down at him like the eyes of giant insects, he replied hesitantly, briefly, to questions that revealed he was a three-dollar-an-hour, part-time delivery boy for a liquor store in Manhattan and a sophomore at Lehman College, City University of New York.

"Will you quit your job?" he was asked.

"I don't know," he said.

"What are you going to do with the money?"

"I haven't thought about it."

After several minutes of equally informative conversation, lottery officials escorted Johnson off the stage and over to the stadium's dining area, which was canopied with a huge red-and-white-striped circus tent. The young man sat down with his arms folded and eyes downcast as though girding himself for the renewed onslaught of reporters and cameramen who'd followed him there.

Cameramen urged him to stand and raise his arms in a gesture of exultation, but when he tried, his expression failed to convey any overt joy. Newsmen fumbled for ways to make Johnson open up and gush forth with reactions and plans for his new fortune, but their efforts were largely fruitless. "My reaction is surprise and serious amazement at the people here," Johnson observed. "I'm still kind of shocked. I mean, you know what I mean."

After a while, as the reporters dispersed to file their stories, an attorney representing the New York State Lottery eased himself into a chair beside Johnson and began conferring with him in monotones, counseling the young man to get an annuity policy, find a good tax advisor, and make out a will. Johnson nodded noncommittally. Soon other lottery representatives joined the attorney and Johnson at the table.

Standing off by himself several feet away from all the

commotion, an elderly black man in a soiled white apron who worked as a cook for the restaurant watched the proceedings in silence. The strain of a lifetime of hard work was etched on his face. He limped as he edged a few feet closer to get a better look at the young man who had become an instant millionaire. Then, shaking his head, the old man said aloud, to no one in particular, "I buy lottery tickets *all* the time."

Like millions of other people, Ed Henry, a 40-year-old dispatcher for the telephone company in Morristown, New Jersey, bought lottery tickets with some regularity—not every week, but when he felt lucky, which was almost every week. Ed and his 24-year-old wife Kathy lived within a tight budget, but he earned a decent salary and took pride in providing for his family. Still, they could afford only one car, and with a third child due soon, they were beginning to outgrow their home. On weekends they looked longingly at the new, bigger houses in a developing suburb close by, but they knew those were beyond their means.

One day at work, a man who dealt in lottery tickets came into the dispatch room and heaped a pile of tickets for the new, million-dollar lottery on one of the desks. Anybody who wanted one just went over and picked out a ticket and paid for it. Henry felt lucky. He selected a ticket.

And, it soon proved, it was a lucky ticket, worth at the very least $500. More important, it was one of 115 that advanced its owner to the finals in the first New Jersey Million Dollar Lottery.

Ed Henry studied the people gathered in the large auditorium for the final drawings. Usually a relaxed, easygoing person, he was beginning to feel the tension of competing with the other finalists. The odds were long—115 to 1. He shifted his eyes systematically from face to face, studying the others in the Trenton War Memorial Building, trying to figure out if anybody looked lucky enough to beat him out of a million dollars.

He had been girding himself for this drawing for weeks. He and his wife Kathy talked continually about what winning would mean to them, to the realization of their hopes for the future. Henry looked at his wife seated beside him. Even though eight months pregnant, she still looked girlish in her sleeveless black maternity dress with its big white collar and black bow. There was so much more he wanted to give her and the kids. This chance of winning a million had almost become an obsession since he became a finalist. His stomach knotted. What would happen now if he didn't win after they'd built their hopes so high? They'd already been spending the money in their minds. It could be a serious disappointment if all this came to nothing.

One by one the names of nine runner-up winners were called, each of these people winning prizes ranging from $10,000 to $200,000. Just one more prize was left, and that was the jackpot. Henry began to rationalize that even if he didn't win the million, he'd still go home five hundred dollars richer, because that would be the consolation prize for all the 105 finalists not winning any of the bigger money.

The names of the remaining finalists were being juggled around in little white plastic balls inside a big transparent ball, and in just seconds, one person out of the 106 remaining contenders was going to be named. Silently, Henry rooted for himself. Even at the horse races he felt he helped his horse along by rooting for it. The governor of New Jersey, who was officiating, picked up one of the balls and Henry's eyes froze on that small, white plastic sphere. Then he heard the words, like a modern-day magic incantation granting his every wish—"Ed Henry!"

As if afraid they'd change their minds, Henry raced up to the stage. He was in a state of shock, of euphoria, but suddenly forty reporters were shoving microphones at him, asking questions, and he "came to." "Take hold of yourself," he told himself. "Say as little as possible."

Mrs. Henry hadn't moved. She sat paralyzed with shock. People all around her were yelling congratulations. As though in a dream, she heard her husband calling her name from the stage. Still she sat, as though rooted to the chair. Finally she managed to get to her feet. Suddenly the tension and joy welling inside her gushed to the surface and the young housewife burst into tears. She cried all the way to the stage, and when Henry saw her, he cried too.

The Henrys laugh now when they recall that one of the first letters they received after winning the lottery jackpot said: "What are you crying for, you boob? You just won a million!"

Ed and Kathy Henry sat in the den of the "dream home" they bought after their win on March 17, 1971, and talked about how their lives had been affected in the years that had since passed.

Ed Henry is a "just folks" kind of guy with a New Jersey accent, thick, wavy, graying hair, a quick, playful grin, and a hearty laugh. He's got the amiable kind of face you'd pick out of a crowd if you needed to ask directions. Dressed comfortably in a red and white checkered shirt and brown slacks, he mixed drinks at his bar in the couple's dark-wood paneled den. Easing himself into a cushiony gold chair, he propped his feet on a big matching ottoman and called his wife in from the kitchen. She sat on a couch across the room from him.

Mrs. Henry, a sweet-voiced, slim young woman with short, brown hair framing her pretty, delicate features, wore blue jeans, a blue and white checked top, and blue sandals. She seemed content to leave Henry center stage in the conversation. And he always turned to her for her reaction when he told anecdotes. She was a good audience.

Their nine-room colonial home in Morristown, New Jersey, occupies a third of an acre of green lawn, similar to the surrounding homes in a neighborhood of trees, station wagons, and the families of successful people. It's as neat a package as Mrs. Henry herself, attractive yet unprepossessing.

Sipping his drink, Henry recalled how the even flow of their lives began to surge over new terrain immediately after their big win.

"We received a check for $50,000 the first day," Henry said. "We were determined from the start that we weren't going to let the money change us much.

"I had our phone number changed even before we got home that day. When we approached our house I saw reporters all over, camping outside. So we sneaked into a neighbor's house and spent the night there. We just couldn't face any more questions and excitement that day."

The following day, when Henry walked into his office, he found it decorated with streamers, signs, and posters to celebrate his win. The signs said, "Mr. Ed $$$$ Henry," "1,000,000," "Daddy Warbucks"; and a poster with pictures of a fancy car, yacht, champagne declared, "This Won't Change My Life One Bit. E.H."

Henry recalled: "My winning blew the lid off the phone company in New Jersey with all the lost man-hours and everybody calling everyone else to talk about it. My phone at work never stopped ringing. And I called my whole family. Everybody was thrilled that someone they knew won. A few weeks after I won I took the whole office out for dinner, about 25 people.

"First thing when you win you feel very benevolent," Henry said. "It was difficult for me to say no to people. But naturally we had to, with all the people asking for money. We helped members of our own family."

When the couple won, Henry was earning $14,000 a year. They'd been shopping for a larger home, but the one they really liked was just a pipe dream on Henry's salary. The lottery money enabled them to buy the house they wanted, enlist the services of a decorator and furnish it. Mrs. Henry got a new station wagon, the thing she wanted most. They helped Henry's parents buy a home in Florida, then spent six weeks vacationing there, and Henry treated himself to some new golf clubs.

They also put a lot of their money away for the future. Henry even went to school at night to learn about stocks and bonds and then made "some pretty good investments."

"We have a busier social schedule now than before. We don't have to hesitate about spending money on baby-sitters and going out. Friends call us and we go here and there. It's nice for Kathy. I was kidding her this morning. I said, 'You haven't cooked on a weekend in the last three months.'

"And I've found the new friends I've made that have more money than my old friends are not different from them. They have the same problems everybody does."

Henry's taking things easier around the house since winning, too. He said, "I never cared for gardening, so now we have a gardener. I eat more and better now." He grinned, patting his stomach, and said, "I've gained about fifteen pounds. Kathy plays golf once a week at the country club we joined, and she takes the kids swimming up there almost every day. She has a good life," he added with pride.

Their spending was hardly in the yacht and champagne class, notwithstanding the comic poster Henry had found in his office after winning. But what they did buy was the stuff of dreams to them.

Mrs. Henry recalled, "That station wagon was one of the few things I really wanted." She also started having someone come in once a week to clean the house. She had tried hiring a live-in maid but that was a short-lived indulgence. Mrs. Henry's independent nature got the better of her after just three months. "The maid was too good," she complained. "She'd be cooking breakfast in the morning and I wanted to do it. I got very bored with nothing to do. I need the self-satisfaction of doing my job."

At the mention of self-satisfaction, Henry looked up in a way that revealed he was aware of one loss the lottery windfall imposed by its very nature. He was a man who took pride in his role as provider. His job, all his efforts, had been dedicated to improving his family's lot in life. They had more now than ever before, but he hadn't earned it. It came from luck, not from him. The lottery had deprived him of that.

Henry admitted he had been questioning lately whether or not he should go on working at the telephone company, or anywhere else for that matter. "I know some million-dollar lottery winners quit their jobs," he pointed out. "I think about quitting every morning. But if I didn't work, what would I do? I don't think it would be good for the kids to have a father who is home all the time. If it was just me and my wife, I probably would quit. But with the kids you have to think about college costs going up every year."

Henry admits his career may really have ended when he won. He shook his head thoughtfully, "I think my initiative is not what it used to be, as a result of winning the million. I'm still with the phone company and now I've switched to data processing. I've had regular salary raises too. But, I haven't moved to any upward position. I don't know whether it's just my personality or what. Maybe I don't perform as well. I don't know whether I'm still putting out a hundred percent."

He complained, "On the job I get a lot of 'Why are you working?' attitudes from some people. If they come up to irritate me they walk away irritated. I ignore it. I shake it off. I know this sort of thing has affected some other million-dollar winners. Some left their jobs. They started getting paranoid, wondering what other people were saying.

"From talking to other million-dollar winners at gatherings we've been to I've found if they're somewhere in their middle years they keep their jobs, but if they're close to retirement, they're more likely to quit.

"We thought of moving to Florida after we won," said Henry. "But in New Jersey we don't have to pay state taxes on our winnings, and in Florida we would. The money we'd lose with such a move is an important consideration to us."

The Henrys both come from lower middle-class backgrounds, and Ed grew up during the Depression. They are cautious about money. As for their kids, Henry said, "We try not to spoil them or give them too much." To Mrs. Henry, what really counts about their windfall is the children's security. "If anything happens to us, the children will be taken care of. I know now the kids can have the best education possible."

These jackpot winners feel they haven't changed much as people despite the giant step in money. Mrs. Henry, chin in hand, mulled over the question of whether there were any changes in herself and said, "I might be a little more outspoken now."

Henry added: "One way I think I've changed is I have less desire to sell myself to people. Now I don't much give a damn. There's a feeling of self-reliance."

It's obvious the Henrys don't count the $50,000 check from the state each year as their greatest riches. Henry stressed, "I don't think the money brings you any more happiness, although it brings a few more goodies. I don't see where a million can hurt a marriage, either. It takes a lot of pressure off, bills and things. But we were happy before. We had everything of what really mattered. And we're happy now."

Dear Lottery Winner:

How are you and all your family? Fine I hope. I saw in the paper that you won a million. Congratulations. Take good care of yourself and family with it. Give a few dollars to the Catholic Church.

And could you please send me a grand so I can get married and have two precious, beautiful kids? I'll pay you back when I get my thirty-four grand from the U.S. Army in about three months. I swear on the blood of Christ to pay you back. I'm a forty-year-old, honest, sincere Irish Catholic. I have never been married although I'm not a virgin.

Please answer soon so I can make love under the moon. God bless you.

The letter was one of the first to arrive after the big night of winning the lottery, a relatively harmless letter, but one of thousands that deluge the homes of lottery winners starting the very morning after.

Harassment by mail and phone is one of many problems with which new lottery winners have to deal. Almost all winners complained of being swamped with mail, including pleas and threats from near and far. There are hard-luck stories, pleas for donations, crackpot investment schemes, loan requests, marriage proposals, absurd advice, and obvious con games to be sorted out from the regular mail and the welcome congratulations of friends and relatives. In batches arrive the poorly scrawled beggings of destitute people who write that they have no food for their children, no eyeglasses, no teeth, no roof over their head, or they will lose a limb or life if this letter, their last hope, goes unanswered. The tragic stories, often appealing to the lottery winner as a fellow member of the working class, haunt the newly rich. Other letters that issue firm demands for money with overt or implied threats ("We will be watching you") frighten them.

"A lot of people wrote to me on the back of overdue electric bills or gas bills. Some of them just sent the bills," said one new lottery millionaire.

The new lottery winner finds that his telephone will ring all the first night unless he takes it off the hook; even the next day, after an unlisted number is secured, the calls somehow continue to trickle in. Obscene telephone calls. Angry attacks by nonwinners and cranks. Strangers are seen loitering around outside the homes of winners. Burglaries occur. There is a good deal of fear.

Some of the winners feel forced into a state of siege. Moving away to isolated residences, they live a guarded life that often brings fear and loneliness.

"My wife is still very upset," said one lottery winner, whispering so that she would not hear. "We're so nervous we can't sleep nights." He had won the New Jersey lottery three years before and had moved to Florida, where the family lived more like fugitives than millionaires.

"We were just talking about a woman who was kidnapped," the man said. "We're afraid. You don't know what kind of kooks might be out there. They might even try to kidnap our kids. Please don't print our name or tell anyone what city we settled in, please!"

One Maryland woman, Rosa Grayson, who had won $400 a week for life, felt fearful too. "I'm just going to pack up and leave," she said. "I have to. People are so mean. You have no idea!"

In the Baltimore suburb of LaPlata, one young woman shut herself inside her white brick home for a long time after winning the million-dollar prize. Her mother said, "My daughter's nerves were never too good, but they're worse now than ever. She thinks someone's gonna hurt her."

Another lottery winner, a young man, came home one night to find suspicious pry marks on his door jamb and thought there were other signs of a break-in. He started carrying a gun.

A bachelor who lived in an apartment complained he was often awakened at three or four o'clock in the morning by strangers pacing outside his door, even pounding on it.

A Chicago woman related: "I was in a bar with a friend when a stranger started swearing and screaming at me because I had the money and I was still working. I was depriving someone of a job, he yelled."

If the reaction of strangers often is frightening to the new lottery winners, the attitudes of others closer to home can be equally upsetting. Friends, neighbors, and co-workers might begin to act differently. Relatives who are not given what they consider a proper share of the winnings often become bitter and estranged.

Teenaged winner Bob Netto of upstate New York mourned: "I never see some of my friends anymore. I think they thought by hanging around with me, other people would think they were trying to be leeches."

A Chicago winner said: "We lost a few friends. They just stopped comin' around. No words were said. I guess they resented us winning."

"We got to know who our real friends are," said lottery winner William Brajczewski of Bristol, Connecticut. "They are the ones who didn't have their hands out."

Eric Leek, a New Jersey big winner, said: "A lot of people I've just met go around professing to be my friend. You've got to be sure who your real friends are."

One million-dollar winner who had liked the old house he lived in before the win said philosophically: "The neighbors and people down the street who used to talk to us got very quiet when we'd go by, and my wife always felt that people were talking about her. They seemed to feel that we were rich so we didn't belong in this kind of neighborhood anymore. So finally we just felt too uncomfortable and we moved." They moved to an upper-middle-class suburb—where they felt equally uncomfortable.

One of the million-dollar winners had been sold the lucky ticket by his sister. In the first flush of congratulations, the winner blurted out to reporters that he was going to give her a tenth of it—not realizing that after taxes were deducted, this would take all of his winnings for perhaps the first three years. Then he tried to correct himself, saying he'd give her $10,000, but the sister broke off with him, angered at the reduction in her gift.

In Deckerville, Michigan, two tavern buddies, Norman Fletcher and Jim Lewis, who had often divided the loot from smaller lottery prizes, vowed friendship even after Fletcher's lottery ticket netted him $1 million. They divided Fletcher's annual checks equally for the first three years, but then there was a falling out and Fletcher refused to continue splitting the money. The lifelong pals ended up fighting in court.

Two New York co-workers who often shared the price of a weekly lottery ticket bought them separately one week. When one of them was declared the winner of a large sum, the other expected half and took the dispute to court, severing their relationship permanently.

An Illinois lottery winner, who had promised before the fact that if he won he'd buy a close relative a new car, carried out his promise with alacrity, only to find that he'd estranged all the other relatives who did not get cars as a gift.

Those who do try to live up to the gift expectations of family members frequently regret it. The winner of a big lottery prize often stops work and since his heavily taxed winnings come in installments, he has to be careful not to give away too many pieces and thus end up financially strained. Take, for example, one man who hit the jackpot in Massachusetts. He proceeded generously to give away so much to his four children, thirteen grandchildren, and eight brothers and sisters that he didn't have enough left to pay his taxes. Instead of living a life of ease, he spent his first year hounded by bill collectors. "We're not really millionaires," he protested. "The money comes in a little at a time, and the government wants half of it."

Most of the million-dollar winners who did not enjoy their jobs before quit them right after winning—and why not, when federal income taxes cut their pre-lottery take-home pay by half? Those who do want to return to work often must weather a barrage of biting humor or outright resentment from co-workers.

"I felt they resented me," said a New Jersey secretary. "They would let me hear comments about people who take jobs they don't really need when others do need them. I wanted to work. I wouldn't know what to do with myself otherwise. But I had to change jobs."

Almost every lottery winner who returns to his or her job runs into a predictable array of practical jokes. They might be called "Mr. Money Bags" or "Miss Money Bags." Their desks are heaped with play money. If there is an "S" in their name, it will be spelled with dollar signs. Attitudes toward them do change. They are the same persons doing the same job, yes, but there is now a big difference. The other workers are there because they *have* to be. The lottery winners work only because they want to.

In balance, those who are really motivated to continue to work generally survive the jibes of co-workers. Many of those who quit their jobs later expressed regret. One millionaire trucker declared: "I really miss that truck driving. The biggest loss of my life is not having someone to tell me what to do."

Especially in cases where people have worked regularly for ten years or more, the idea of doing nothing all day long presents a fearful void in their lives. The comment was often repeated, "What would I do with myself?" Only those who were close to retirement age, in their fifties or sixties, expressed no loss in the idea of voluntary unemployment.

It may be socially acceptable to retire early, but for younger men or women to elect not to work seems repugnant in our culture, especially for males. There's more to it than just the fear of being mistaken for someone unable or unwilling to get a job and therefore perhaps lazy, unskilled, or ignorant. For years a man has had to convince himself that it is absolutely necessary that he rise and go to work each day, that he is needed on the job by his employer and by his family. Suddenly this mandatory routine is no longer necessary, and in its absence is a day totally lacking in structure and purpose.

Curiously, whichever route the new millionaires chose, working or not working, there was no sign that either group was better prepared to handle the practice of leisure. Everyone desires a certain amount of leisure, and it's an ultimate goal of our system, but few people eagerly face sustained leisure, not even those who suddenly can afford it. We spend our lives pursuing money and security, but when we get it, the problem of no longer having to struggle presents a more formidable problem than the struggle itself.

Similarly, although "rising to a higher level" of society serves as another powerful motivation of work effort, there may be an argument against too much rising in the fact that those new lottery millionaires who purchased homes far beyond their former economic bracket seldom felt they fit in with their new neighbors or even the physical surroundings themselves. If the lottery winners purchased homes in remote places in an effort to flee the harassment of neighbors, they would often isolate themselves from their new neighbors as well. If they were just attempting to buy the best home they could now afford, they frequently did not feel accepted: they hadn't earned their wealth as their neighbors had; they didn't feel entitled to the same social status.

Of course, there are numerous exceptions to all the complaints voiced by lottery winners. For every situation that some regarded as intolerable, there were other winners who dismissed the same problem with a shrug or overcame the difficulty with ease.

The unruffled Ed Henry handled press harassment by speaking openly with any and all reporters, always making himself available even though—as the nation's first million-dollar lottery winner—he bore the brunt of inquiries for some time. As for the hate mail, the crank letters, he just threw away the envelopes that appeared erratic. And while bothered by pleas in what might be genuine cases of tragic need, he was able to accept that no individual could possibly distinguish the genuine ones from the bogus, and even then one couldn't personally solve them all, no matter how prosperous.

There are many people who adapt to the problems of new wealth without missing a stride. Mrs. Malden Blough, a middle-aged housewife in rural Holsapple, Pennsylvania, is married to a steel mill worker who retired at 52 when he won a million. The Bloughs spent prudently. Commented Mrs. Blough: "We try not to live beyond the level that we were always used to. If we did we'd be out of place. What would our friends say?"

Tony Califano of Long Island, New York, who won a gigantic $980,000 lump sum, kept on working despite having to take a lot of kidding from co-workers. Before the windfall, the Califanos were average, hard-working people, living from week to week, trying to pay their bills and somehow to fit in extra expenses like remodeling the bathroom. After winning, Califano shopped around for a bargain in a Ford; when a real estate agent showed them a $97,000 house, he said, "That's not me." His wife agreed: "We wouldn't be happy there."

Another million-dollar winner, when asked about the deluge of mail and harassment by suspicious people, replied: "What mail? What harassment? Nobody's bothered me."

He was a uniformed policeman, William Inman of Peoria, Illinois.

In North Arlington, New Jersey, Eric Leek, a 26-year-old barber and hair stylist, had a lot going for him. Tall and good-looking, with a slender build, moustache, and semi-beard, he had a live-in girlfriend, a nice roomy apartment, and an active life. Next door to the barbershop where he worked lottery tickets were sold, and it was there that Leek purchased forty tickets one week; one of them landed him one of the most profitable lottery prizes ever awarded.

Because of the Bicentennial in 1976, the state of New Jersey had prepared that year a special lottery based on the date 1776: that amount in dollars would be paid to the grand prize winner every week for life. It would total about $92,000 a year. If Eric Leek won, he stood to collect more than $3 million by the time he was 60, and if he lived to be 90, almost another $3 million. (It was a record-high lottery prize at the time, but within a year it was to be topped by Massachusetts.)

In the crowded Montclair State College auditorium, where the drawing was held, Leek leaped to his feet when his name was announced as the lucky winner. He hugged his girlfriend Mathilde, who had taken the day off from her bookkeeper's job in New York to accompany him, and led her to the stage, arm around her waist. She was so nervous she could barely stand. They told the crowd they were engaged to be married in June, but in view of the fantastic lottery prize, Mathilde called out unsurely, "Is there a preacher in the house?"

Leek told the audience he was going to church to thank the Lord, he'd build a youth center, give his parents a home in the country, and pursue a career as a gospel singer. "I hope to use the money working for the betterment of mankind," he said. "Praise the Lord, I hope I can help a lot of people." Then he proceeded to celebrate with Chivas Regal Scotch and fried chicken and a suite in the Great George Hotel in northern New Jersey. It was a wild celebration, and why not? Leek had just won the biggest lottery prize in the two hundred years of a benevolent America.

Almost two years later Leek was still single, living in a luxurious apartment in Hackensack, proud of his rosewood furniture and two Jaguars. He'd traveled to Europe, Mexico, the Caribbean, all over America. As for the youth center he wanted to build, the town officials opposed the idea. Nobody wanted a bunch of hyperactive teenagers in their neighborhood. His parents rejected his offer of a new home; they liked the one they had. And his former bride-to-be, well, that's all over now, although Leek said, "We're still in touch." She complained, "He thinks he's in another league now."

Despite an eventful year of globe-trotting, horseback riding, scuba diving, and flying, Leek insisted, "The money hasn't changed my life. . . . In some cases there's a change in women's reaction to me because of the money, but I've always attracted them. I've never had any problems. I guess I'm more guarded now with women because of the money. The first year or so it was kind of hard to get my act together. There were a lot of women. But basically now it's one or two.

"Now it's a completely different lifestyle. I'm more secure now than I was before. The money has given me creature comforts. I've become somewhat of a recluse."

He showed a little anger at himself and the whole lottery fame situation, and he wasn't afraid to say what he felt. "For about a year and a half it was pretty hard to live with all these people coming to me with schemes on what to do with my money. I made all the wrong moves at first. I hired the best lawyers, the best accountants, the best bankers, and as far as I'm concerned they weren't worth beans, I just feel it was all bull____. I don't see any need for it. One lawyer warned me that if I continued as a hair stylist I could be sued by someone who said I damaged their hair. What bull! If someone wanted to sue me for something like that they'd have a hard time. I like hair-styling and I still do it occasionally.

"The heaviest thing with winning a million is the identity crisis—after 26 years of your life suddenly becoming catapulted to an entirely different existence. You question yourself. What are you going to do with your life? What is the money going to do for you? What do you really want? Are you going to change your life? That's the biggest pitfall.

"If I knew at the time I won the lottery what I know now, I would have avoided the press completely and split to another city or state. The biggest problem is this catapult into the limelight. You get fame with the money, and it's twice as heavy.

"I've settled down now. Money hasn't changed my ambition. My ambition was to open up a hair-styling shop, pursue my singing career. I'm a vocalist and I've written songs. I've bought some recording equipment, I've done a lot of practicing, and I've even appeared as a singer in a few small nightclubs where they didn't know I'm a lottery winner. I'd eventually like to have my own nightclub.

"I'm religious and I have prayed for guidance. I turn to prayer all the time, and there's no question the prayer helped.

"There's nothing more powerful than the almighty dollar," Leek said. "But as far as happy goes, you can't buy happiness. Money just brings a different set of problems."

When the big party was over, the man was both a winner and a loser. Police found him slumped over the wheel of an allegedly stolen New York Transit Authority bus, a half-empty vodka bottle in one hand, and in his pocket a ticket claiming a $5,000 prize in the million-dollar lottery drawing held the previous night at Roseland Dance City. There, entertainer Jerry Lewis had presented the grand prize of $1,000 a week for life to another New Yorker, 26-year-old John Sartoretti, who worked as a telephone equipment installer in the Wall Street area.

"Did you see my name in the paper?" said the drunken man as police roused him from his slumber at the wheel of the empty bus he had "borrowed" after becoming impatient at waiting for the regular service. As he was led away at three A.M. to spend the rest of the night at the Bronx House of Detention, he kept repeating, "I won the lottery."

Police verified that in fact the man had been one of 83 lucky holders of tickets that spelled out the word "Jackpot." A crowd of hundreds of spectators had filled the dance hall auditorium to watch the division of luck, with one of the 83 chosen for the jackpot, three runners-up awarded $25,000 each, five others getting $10,000, and the remaining 74—including the unauthorized bus driver—getting a mere $5,000.

Some 25 million tickets on that drawing had been torn up before the big party even started, although thousands more had been redeemed for prizes ranging downward from $1,000 to $5.

The question that hung in the sobering air of the morning after had to do with luck. Was the jailed $5,000 winner lucky for having won that much, or was he unlucky because he had lost the million-dollar top prize?

Meanwhile, in Chicago, they considered William Thompson a lucky man. He had just hit the Illinois Bonanza for $200,000. Thompson, a black man from Arkansas, had moved to the Chicago ghetto years before in hopes of escaping the drudgery of pre-Civil Rights Dixie life. It had been far from smooth going, but he'd been married forty years and had managed to raise eight children. Disabled in an automobile accident, he hadn't worked a day in the last seven years, living instead on a meager monthly disability check. He promised to use his bonanza to fix up the house, buy his wife a new sofa and a coat, and get the kids—the youngest now thirteen—some school clothes. For himself, all he wanted was a camper van. Now, of course he was lucky. But he might have appreciated a little luck earlier in life, too.

"I kind of expected I was going to win," said Thompson, without specifying what in the previous six decades had led him to believe he was one of fortune's favorites.

When Eric Leek, the New Jersey hair stylist, was decreed a winner, he made a similar statement after thanking the Lord. "I had a feeling I was going to win," he said. "I was picked as the number ten finalist and I was born on the tenth hour of the tenth day of the tenth month, and I met my girl on the tenth day of the month."

By some formula or another, most people believe that Lady Luck constantly watches over them and that, when it really counts, she won't let them down. The mind tends to apply this secret resource, this Ace up the Sleeve, this magic force kept in reserve, equally to horse races and fears of mortality.

Coaxing Lady Luck out of her shadows and into action requires tricks which most people employ with varying degrees of consciousness. Finalists in one lottery drawing were polled by a newspaper reporter who found that a majority wore "lucky new shoes" in the belief that, well, it might help, or at least it wouldn't hurt.

The ritual of touching, reflecting a primitive belief in what is known as "sympathetic magic," was experienced by most lucky winners. In the belief that some of their luck could "rub off" onto others, winners were besieged by crowds who wanted to touch them or have them touch their lottery tickets. Said one winner, a high school girl who had returned to school the next day, "I looked at myself that night and I was covered all over with little bruises from being touched."

Our offerings to the great Giver of Gifts are often merely symbolic gestures, but they are nevertheless widespread. After winning a million dollars in the Ohio State Lottery, truck driver Dale Weber, 51, of Upper Sandusky, recalled the tension of the drawing: "I'm not superstitious," he insisted, "but I had my fingers crossed so hard they were turning white."

Religious faith is often regarded as a private ally where luck is concerned. When her husband won a million-dollar prize, teenaged Judy Netto confided. "This is what did it," fingering a small wooden statue of the Virgin Mary she had carried to the drawing in her purse.

Mrs. Anna Mizerak of Little Falls, New York, won the million-dollar prize after seven decades of hard life and murmured to herself over and over as she was led to the winner's circle, "A miracle, miracle, miracle."

In Peoria, Illinois, policeman William Inman explained his million-dollar luck: "I personally believe in God, and I personally believe He did it. I just wonder, kinda, why out of all these people God had to pick me. . . . He probably had His reasons."

Mrs. Eunice M. Schiller of Randallstown, Maryland, a secretary who became another million-dollar winner, said: "I'm a living example that the Lord answers prayers. I don't believe in luck. I've been praying for five months, and my prayers have been answered. Somebody loves me upstairs."

It's no coincidence that Luck is a lady, according to psychiatrists. Their interpretation of why most people feel that luck will not forsake them returns to infancy. When we are babies, our hunger and distress are solved for us by the appearance of Mother, a figure looming out of the skies above. As we grow, we learn that fulfilling our desires is no longer so simple, but instead requires considerable effort on our own part. We adapt to this, but always we retain in the back of our minds a yearning for the lovely days when we were so lucky that, just when we happened to hunger, along came a breast.

"Everybody feels secretly that they are the seventh son of the seventh son, the child of fortune," observed psychoanalyst Dr. Wahl in considering the comments of lottery winners. Dr. Wahl explained that even though common sense tells us otherwise, we not only believe in luck, but we surround the belief with little rituals. "As proof that people believe in luck, we need only point out that Las Vegas exists. Out of every fifty people who go there, only one wins money gambling, but the city prospers because everybody believes that he will be the one to defy the odds."

Concerning the rituals we practice, Dr. Wahl told of a patient who, as a G.I. during World War II just before the Normandy invasion, feeling that he had nothing to lose, began to gamble, playing cards recklessly. The more daringly he played, the more he won and won and won. When the game ended, he had amassed $70,000. But now he began to suffer a great anxiety. Now that he did have something to lose, he felt certain that he'd be killed in the D-Day battle. So he found himself another card game and played until he lost the entire sum. Broke again, he went into the invasion with a light heart—and came through it unharmed.

"It's ancient," Dr. Wahl said, but we still have this feeling that the gods envy humans their happiness and must be appeased or we will suffer their wrath." To this he attributed the frequent avowals of lottery winners that they will do something to benefit mankind, will donate to the poor, will go to church and pray, will henceforth lead in short, an exemplary life, lest the gods revoke their favor. So the people who deluge a new lottery winner with pleas for alms are following ancient ritual, too, sensing that the recipient of so great a gift must surely feel the immediate need to appease the gods by some selfless act of charity.

Most of the lottery winners are genuinely disturbed to hear through the mails or otherwise, of the ill fortune of so many needy people. But more concrete fears and doubts intervene to block potential donations: principally the traditional American fear of being taken for a sucker. Two teenagers, both of whom had recently won million-dollar lotteries, were talking one afternoon. The youth who had won first advised the newcomer to the ranks of the American Dream Come True: "Don't go with any funny schemes . . . They'll rip you off if you give them the chance."

Tony Califano, a big, round man, took another spoonful of chocolate parfait and nodded his agreement with what the young man across the table was saying. His broad, good-natured face, dominated by his dark hair and moustache, was lit with a genial smile. His burly body in a green leisure suit tilted slightly forward to catch the words above the din of conversation from the 25 people gathered at the horseshoe-shaped table in the fashionable restaurant.

There appeared to be nothing out of the ordinary about the banquet party, and other patrons passing by took little notice of them. The men in the group were for the most part dressed for comfort in sports shirts and slacks, and the women were casual in summery dresses or slacks and tops. The average age was around 40 but there was a teenaged couple and one in their sixties. When their meal was finished, the meeting of the New York Lottery Millionaire's Club, of which all these people were charter members, began its first session. An Alcoholics Anonymous type of meeting organized to give lottery millionaires a chance to share their problems, it differed from most self-help groups in being based not on shattered dreams, but dreams come true.

The group looked more like a family bowling league gathering than an assembly of millionaires. If one of the waitresses scurrying back and forth bearing trays of roast beef, salad, fruit cocktail, and rolls had been asked to pick out a millionaire from among the group, she probably would have vetoed the long-haired kid in the dark blue shirt and the lanky man with the cowboy hat, and chosen instead one of several dapper men in suits seated at the head of the table. But the men in suits, far from being millionaires, were salaried officials of the lottery commision. John D. Quinn, the New York Lottery director, was one of them, and he rose to address the winners:

"We want to meet regularly. We want to know how old winners have solved problems, because that will help us advise new winners. . . ." Quinn, an imposing-looking man who the lottery millionaires jokingly refer to as "Daddy Warbucks" or their "fairy godfather," closed his little talk with a verbal caress: "I'm really pleased with the people who have won. Nice, decent American people. I hope you'll all stay in touch with the lottery."

Some of the children brought along by the lottery winners and seated at a separate table nearby were squirming restlessly before the formal speech-making was done. By the time the last of the parfaits had been whisked off the tables, the meeting had begun to take on the air of a highly select encounter group.

"The press is the worst of it," one millionaire complained to Quinn. "They go too far. I felt I never wanted to do another interview."

"You have to set your own pace," Quinn advised. "But you are in the public domain. Once you win that prize I can't tell the press not to bother you."

"I resented it when I read rumors that my wife and I are breaking up. Once they reported I was in a state hospital. None of it was true."

Another man told how he turned things around and used the press for his benefit, instead of vice versa, "I got myself a discount on a red Cadillac by promising to mention the dealer's name every chance I got."

"After I won," said Califano, "I had an offer from a bank that if I deposited a hundred thousand for a year they'd give me 8 percent interest. But before I'd won, the same bank had turned me down for a loan. So I said, 'Forget it.' Plenty of banks were after me."

"You really have to be careful," said soft-spoken nineteen-year-old Bob Netto. "When you go out to buy things, they see you coming and the price goes up. I started having a family member or my lawyer buy for me when it was something big."

Netto and his teenaged wife Judy, who like to fish and hunt, live in a one-bedroom cottage with an outhouse at Three Mile Bay near Watertown, New York. He's thinking about starting a small marina and renting motorboats, but he admits, "I'm not sure what I want anymore. Before, when I was working in a gas station, I just wanted to become a mechanic. Now a lot more is open to me. But now it's like starting over again."

Netto had quit high school to get married. When he won his million dollars, he and his wife were both working, he at the gas station, she in the local Acme Market. "Working for it is better," he said. "You appreciate it more. But marriage is easier now, with the money pressure off. Judy and me have become closer, but I'm not really any happier now. There are just different pressures."

Several states—including New York, New Jersey, and Illinois—have formed these Millionaire's Clubs, bringing together the lottery winners and special advisors for the problems they face: handling money, investing, taxes, legal matters, to name just a few: To date, none of the groups has taken lessons on how to live with their new wealth from such experts as psychologists, though they have discussed the problems of adapting among themselves.

Ed Henry, the nation's first lottery millionaire, headed the first Millionaire's Club, which started in New Jersey. "We used to get together quite often," Henry said. "We'd usually meet in a restaurant, sometimes in people's homes, but the last year or so the thing got too big. There's too many of them. Kathy used to pitch in calling people, helping set things up and we'd meet every few months, but now there's too much work to it. It's grown too big.

"The first time we met, they telephoned me and invited me to the Millionaire's Club, and I didn't even know we had one, but when I got there they called me up to the head table and told me I was the president, so why didn't I say a few words. I'm no after-dinner speaker, but I got used to it.

"When I gave them advice, the new lottery millionaires, I'd tell them: 'Don't do anything for six months. Just assess the situation. And don't tell anybody what you're going to do until *you* find out exactly what you want to do.'

"But the whole Millionaire's Club idea was the brainchild of the advertising agency, and the main thing it did was give the lottery free publicity. Still, we had some good meetings. They're all very nice people, the members. Oh, there's a couple of them I don't know how to take. One guy I think is strange. But it's a good group."

Richard Smith (a pseudonym), a short but well-muscled young Baltimore resident, had plenty to worry about. At 23 years of age, he was unemployed and had a wife and two children to support. He'd quit his previous job as a forklift operator making less than $2.50 an hour. It had been a lousy job, one of a long line of lousy jobs that never had earned him more than $3,000 a year. He was furious with the state of Maryland because they had refused his application for jobless pay, and now he was faced with the bleak prospect of starting work at the only job available, driving a city garbage truck. He was supposed to start the following Monday.

But Smith had an ace up his sleeve. For the past several weeks he and his wife Sally (a pseudonym), who would be 17 in another month, had been living on the $500 prize he'd recently won. He usually bought two lottery tickets every week, putting one in his name and one in Sally's, and even though they were practically broke that week, she had given him a dollar out of her grocery money and he had gotten the lucky ticket.

The ticket turned out worth more than the $500, because it qualified Smith for the finals, which meant a chance at a half dozen $5,000 prizes and a few even bigger ones. There was a $100,000 prize and the big one, a million. On the night of the drawing, in 1974, he combed his unbarbered hair and trimmed the long sideburns, put on his best shirt, the one with green stripes, and left Sally to baby-sit the kids in the house his father owned. He caught the bus to the expensive Lord Baltimore Hotel, feeling a little uneasy about not wearing a coat or tie, but as he told Sally, "I'm a simple man and I'm going as a simple man."

Sally, who was slender and slightly taller than he, had

long, straight blonde hair and a pleasant face. She accepted it as natural that he should go to the drawing without her. First of all, they didn't have the money for both to go. She wasn't sure she wanted to go, anyway. She didn't have the clothes for a place like that. Sally was used to a tough life. She had first been married when she was thirteen and she'd had a baby right away; then her first husband had been killed in an automobile accident. She'd married Smith when she was fifteen and he'd just gotten out of the Army, and then she'd had another baby. There was never enough money. They hadn't even been able to afford a honeymoon.

Less than three hours after leaving Sally, Smith was declared a millionaire. As he stood in front of the crowd at the Lord Baltimore, and as the Lottery Commission chairman raised Smith's left arm in a fighter's victory gesture, he smiled modestly and lowered his eyes. The lottery director, playing to the crowd, awkwardly hugged Smith's neck to his shoulder in a sort of hammerlock, and Smith's straight brown hair fell across his forehead.

Smith candidly told his story of impoverishment and explained: "I guess I'm basically lazy like everyone else. If I didn't like a job I was working on, I'd just quit." He told about his garbage truck job due to start Monday, adding, "But I don't think I'll be there."

What would he do with the money? He'd buy a car, a nice house, and make some investments, he told the press, but most of all, he wanted to donate $10,000 a year to Vietnamese orphans. "I've always liked kids," he said.

Somebody asked Smith if he wasn't going to telephone his wife with the news. "Can't," he said. "Haven't got a phone." Lottery officials reminded him that he was entitled to use the Millionaire's Suite at the hotel that night. They offered to drive over and pick her up. After some hesitation, he accepted the offer of a lift home, to safeguard the first of his twenty annual checks in the sum of $50,000.

Six months later he was broke. "He was spending on everything, giving it away," his wife recalled. "He bought

everything for everybody except me and the kids." The way
he was going at it, she said, "If they gave us the whole million
in one lump it still would have been gone, all of it."

Smith managed to borrow $10,000 against the next
check and bought an antique shop which he believed would
tide them over until the following March, and when that
check came he had the antique shop auctioned off at a loss so
they could pack up and leave town.

Greenville, Texas, a city of 25,000 people about a
hundred miles northeast of Dallas, was the place they chose for
a fresh start. Greenville, a conservative county seat that had
thrived in the 1800's when cotton was king, and that had
experienced a new spurt of growth with the arrival of the
electronics industry in post-World War II days, retained its
charm through the years, with the big old city homes of
ranchers still lining wide, tree-shaded streets. The Smiths had
visited Greenville once, before the lottery win. Sally's father
and stepmother lived there, on a rural route near town. Smith
had paid off all his bills before he left Baltimore, and all the
loans, too, and after taxes were paid they really weren't starting out the year with $50,000—it was more like half that sum.
But he got some furniture, put a down payment on a new
house, and there they started a new life.

That was in March. In August, Sally, pregnant again,
went to a lawyer's office and declared, "I want a divorce."

The lawyer inquired about her circumstances and she
tearfully spilled out her troubles. She felt he didn't love her
anymore, she said. She felt her marriage was over. She told
the lawyer that as far as she was concerned, Smith could have
everything, the house, the cars, all of it, because she'd lost
him, so she'd lost everything anyway. She didn't want the
house, it had too many bad memories for her.

As for the cost of a divorce, Mrs. Smith said, "I don't
have any money. I don't have any way to pay you."

She hadn't mentioned the lottery winnings at that point
because she wasn't aware that she might have any claim to the
money, but in the course of the conversation with the lawyer,

she just happened to mention that her husband had won a million dollars up in Maryland.

In the fall of 1975, in the Superior Court, Hunt County, Texas, at Greenville, suit was filed against Richard Smith by Sally Smith, petitioning for divorce, custody of the two children, and a division of community property.

Smith left town, returning to Baltimore. By the following spring, Sally Smith, aged nineteen, had been awarded a new house, furnishings, a car, and half of what was still to come of the million. It had been untried ground, but her lawyer won the authority of the Maryland courts to order the Lottery Commission to pay half of all the remaining $50,000 checks to her.

Sally, with custody of the children, now began to make plans for her life. She wanted to apply at the East Texas State University, fifteen miles from Greenville, for a General Education Development test to get the equivalent of a high school diploma, and then she'd go to Licensed Vocational Nursing School right there in Greenville.

She would have to work. She would have to make arrangements for a baby-sitter. As for the checks she'd get in the amount of $25,000 every year, the lawyer who won them for her had taken her case on a contingency basis and she'd agreed to pay $100,000 or $10,000 a year for 10 years as a fee. Taxes would reduce the check to less than $20,000 a year, and the lawyer would get ten of what was left.

When you allow for tax deductions, attorney's fees, and the first $150,000 that had already been squandered, all that was left of the million-dollar bonanza was about one-fourth for each of the divorced couple, to be spread thin over seventeen remaining years.

The nursing school plans never worked out. Soon townspeople were observing Mrs. Smith "hot-shotting" around town in her car, wearing the skimpiest of cut-off jeans and halter. She started learning to drive an eighteen wheeler, going off on long-distance hauls as an apprentice with another truck driver. She felt she couldn't live in the house that had been awarded to her and had no equity in it, anyway, so she just abandoned it and moved to an apartment in a lower rent district. There was a problem with child care when she had to be out of town.

Her ex-husband meanwhile had returned to Greenville and married a local girl who, like him, had recently been divorced. In the spring of 1976, just after getting the first of his half-checks and paying off debts, he sued his ex-wife for custody of the children, asking for $1,000 a month child support. He got custody of the children, with her consent, and the court ordered her to pay him $200 a month in support. Smith was living in a house on the property of his new wife's father in Greenville with his own children, his ex-wife's daughter, and children from his new wife's former marriage. He still didn't have a job.

One might expect the spending habits of the lottery millionaires to produce a wide range of approaches to the American dream, but the shopping lists of the early winners were surprisingly parochial. Ed Henry bought a Cadillac, a car he'd always wanted. Richard Smith bought two Torinos. Paul McNabb bought a jeep. Tony Califano bought a Ford. Most of them bought new homes, most of them bought new furniture, and most of them went on trips.

"What are we going to do with the money?" a Bronx housewife said. "We're going to get the hell out of the Bronx." Her husband wanted a 30-foot sailboat.

"A trip to Europe," said a Boston secretary. "A chalet in New Hampshire, a new car, and all the children I want."

"Before I won I would have given my right arm for a van," said a teenager. "After I won I decided I didn't want one anymore."

A Baltimore lady said, "We'll take the kids to Disney World, then maybe pay our house off."

Stanley Sapinsky, a New Jersey winner, bought a Cadillac—just walked into a showroom in Hackensack and peeled off the cash for it. He also helped a friend pay off the medical bills for her daughter's brain operation.

Agnes Noweski, a West Keansburg, New Jersey, widow who won a million at age sixty, didn't know what to do with the money. She thought about who would be the wisest, most conservative advisor she could consult and decided to see an elderly, highly respected accountant friend. "Agnes," he told her, "why don't you just piss it away?" Following his advice, she bought a gold Thunderbird, lots of perfume and jewelry and clothes, went on an endless round of ocean cruises, threw lots of parties, and had lots of fun. Why not?

But there are few examples of real extravagance to be found among the lottery millionaires. They seem afraid to display too many traits of the *nouveau riche* and they cling almost desperately to old values. Furs, diamonds, maids, yachts, chauffeurs are almost invariably ignored. For these people, it would appear, conspicuous consumption is dead. They save their money for important things.

The first and most important thing that most of them buy is freedom from debt. With the bonded assurance that there will be big paychecks regularly every year, whether or not they keep their jobs, no matter what happens, they can stop worrying about their children's education, a leaky roof, a hole in the carpet, the cheapest dish on the menu, the knock in the car's overworked engine, and whether they can really afford to go on vacation this year. The comments are unanimous. The smiles are abundant:

"Sure, that's the best part of it, the security. Knowing there'll always be food on the table and that the kids can go to college."

"It's like a great burden was lifted off your shoulders."

"I don't mind going to work anymore, because I know if I don't want to, I don't have to."

"You don't have to worry about the everyday things anymore, like food and rent."

"The main thing I think is to get out of debt and stay out of debt."

"I find that I don't care that much about impressing people anymore. Whether they like me or not doesn't worry me."

"The money gives you independence."

"You can see it on their faces," said a publicity spokesman who meets annually with the lottery millionaires at check distribution time. "The worry has gone out of their faces. If you compare their faces from before they won, you look at them now and the wrinkles are gone. The worry has gone."

What is the average lottery millionaire like?

These observations on the major purchases of lottery millionaires, as well as their comments, came from an informal survey, conducted by the authors, of fifty persons who won the million-dollar lottery prize in Illinois, Maryland, Massachusetts, New Jersey, New York, Ohio, and Pennsylvania.

The ages of these thirty-six men and fourteen women ranged from 19 to 79, the average being 44. There were eleven single men and six single women. Obviously, with male winners outnumbering females by such a large margin, the statistics can't be interpreted to read that men are luckier or more interested in the lottery, but only that married women often are content to participate vicariously through the tickets their mates buy.

Some curious gaps appear in the age groups of the winners: Two were in their teens, five in their twenties, fourteen in their thirties, eight in their forties, thirteen in their fifties, five in their sixties and three in their seventies. It appears that there are many more winners in their thirties and fifties than any other age group. But it can also be observed that twenty-one of the winners were under 40 and the same number were between 40 and 60 years of age.

The conservative behavior of the majority of winners, as noted in their sensible spending, repeats itself in their work habits. Twenty out of forty-two who were employed continued working at the same job or a similar one after winning, although some reduced their hours. Twenty-two quit work, but nine of these indicated they wanted to return part-time or prepare for full-time work in a better job. Eight were unemployed when they won, but these included three retired men and two elderly women. Of the thirteen winners who quit their jobs and voiced no plans to resume work, ten were 50 years of age or older.

Considering that money was no longer a motivation for working, and that the tax situation would mean they'd actually be working for less money than before, this high degree of dedication to work comes as something of a surprise, all the more so when job categories are reviewed. Only eight of the winners in the survey worked in professions such as teacher, artist, executive, and small business owner, where personal satisfaction is frequently a major work incentive. The others were secretaries, clerks, waitresses, and blue-collar workers. Of five secretaries who won, for example, four planned to continue work and the fifth wanted to stay home and have children. Two out of three steel workers who won returned to the mills. One of the two quit for a time but returned after a few months of intolerable idleness.

"What would I do with myself if I quit work?" was the way many of the lottery winners expressed it. As one secretary put it: "I'd go nuts."

The average lottery millionaire—to summarize our survey—is a 44-year-old married man from the East Coast (where million-dollar prizes started) with slightly more than two children. After winning he continues to work, and with his lottery money he buys a new house and car, goes on a trip, and allows himself and his family such other small indulgences as furniture, clothes, and recreation. A portrait of this average winner doesn't have to be drawn any more clearly, since the statistics almost perfectly match Ed Henry of New Jersey at the time he won. The vast majority of lottery winners, like Henry, do not greatly alter their lives, but rather upgrade their standard of living and set themselves free of the widespread financial insecurities that beset the white- and blue-collar workers who form the ranks of lottery ticket buyers.

Lottery "millionaires" aren't really millionaires after all. They receive only about $30,000 a year or more, depending on their tax situation. Since most of them already are employed, their "bonanza" often represents only a tripling or sometimes only a doubling of their annual income. That may be a dream devoutly to be wished, yet it is one within the scope of ordinary reality—not a head-spinning, bottomless-bank-balance realm of fantasy.

Very few really ran wild. The few who tried quickly discovered the finite nature of their installment-plan fortune. Undoubtedly, if (like John Beresford Tipton's no-strings gifts in the televised fiction series of the 1950's, "The Millionaire") the states bestowed their million-dollar prizes in one lump sum, tax-free, the illusion of great wealth would prompt more lottery winners to throw caution to the winds, with unpredictable results. But, for better or worse, they don't.

Nevertheless, the wisdom of the states (who knew better than to give whiskey to the Indians, too) doesn't entirely account for the sober handling of money by the lottery winners, and that is to the winners' own credit. Perhaps they recognize that the old, solid, middle-class values they have always lived by are closer to what they want than any fantasy-land existence they cannot, in any case, really afford. Most of the troubles that confront the lottery winners come not from the money itself, but from the attendant fame, which the lottery operators manipulate to serve their own interests. It's a business to them, with a profit motive, even if the profit does enrich the state treasury. But as the lottery millionaire, scenario is repeated time and again, the fame, and the troubles, are likely to diminish.

When an unemployed parent in Maryland hit the jackpot, headline writers tagged the story:

JOBLESS FATHER BEATS SYSTEM

Not really. The lottery has become part of the system, and that new lottery millionaire hasn't beaten the system, he's joined it. By becoming part of a multimillion-member group created to serve the interests of the state, and by being luckier than others in the group, he's helping to sell more lottery tickets to the winners and losers of the future. The big lottery winners, after all, are not the individuals who take home lottery prizes, but rather the states that hand them out.

But, so far, no one seems to mind.

2. Easy Come...

Jolene Gearin felt despondent; exactly why, she didn't know. She sat in the kitchen of her small apartment, staring out into the old harbor where work-stained tankers and rusted freighters of half a dozen flags were moored. Long Beach is the seaport of Los Angeles, and its old docks and weathered waterfront resemble seaports everywhere. The water was not blue and appealing but it comforted Jolene to watch it because somewhere at another edge of the Pacific was her husband Leonard. This time, he had been gone for years.

She was in her forties, but her blonde hair and bright blue eyes gave her a much younger appearance. In smart clothes, like the blue pant suit she was wearing now—she had made it herself—she knew she was attractive. But life, she felt, was passing her by. For one thing, her birthday had just gone by uncelebrated, not even a card from her husband. And a lonesome Christmas 1966 had just passed, too. He could have called, she brooded, even if he was in Australia.

51

When he married her twenty some years before, he had
been in the merchant marine, and she had soon grown accustomed to his absences. At first it was just a few weeks at a time,
then six weeks at a time, then six months. On the latest trip
he'd been working for Mobil Oil in Australia for nearly three
years.

Her life centered on her small, $75-a-month apartment
and the three teenaged children who still lived with her. The
other two had gone their own way, but still kept in touch.
Once in a while some women friends would pick her up and
take her to the beach, but she had no car of her own, so she
was usually stuck at home.

Money was a problem. There never was enough. She
was allowed to charge the groceries and send the bills to her
husband, but she couldn't shop for the things she really
wanted, like a new rug or couch. She cooked for the kids,
cleaned the house, washed dishes, washed clothes, sewed, and
that was it. Still, she wasn't terribly discontented. She didn't
expect very much out of life.

She would have loved to travel. When the kids would
gather around they'd all say, "If only we had the money,
wouldn't it be great if we took a vacation this year and went up
into the mountains, or to Arizona, or Lake Tahoe?" But they
knew it wouldn't happen.

The telephone rang and she got up and walked the few
steps to the telephone and picked it up. It was an aunt, who
lived several miles away but did not call frequently.

"Did you see the program? Did you see the show?"

"What program?" asked Mrs. Gearin. "What are you
talking about?"

"The Art Linkletter Show," said the aunt impatiently.
"You mean you didn't see it? Your father is dead! You'll get
$200,000!"

It was a bolt of lightning out of the blue, but still there
was something unreal about the whole thing. She couldn't
grasp what her aunt was talking about—the Art Linkletter

Show, her father, $200,000. What did any of these things
have to do with each other?

Mrs. Gearin had not heard from her father for three
years, but that wasn't unusual. He had left when she was a
child. She remembered that he came to see her when she was
twelve years old, and that she had seen him again after her
marriage. When she started having children, he paid a visit
every two years or so. She distinctly recalled that he had always painted a picture of himself being very poor. He was so
thrifty that he once scolded her for setting out too much food
on the lunch table. "Waste, waste, waste," he complained, and
she was stunned because she was doing it just for him. And
now he was dead. She was near tears, remembering how, as a
child, she had wanted to run away and go to Seattle because
she had heard he lived there. The realization that she would
never see him again was beginning to sink in.

On the telephone, her aunt persisted in explaining, and
gradually Mrs. Gearin understood. Art Linkletter, who she
knew as a television personality, had a program that he called
Missing Heirs, which had a private detective trace the relatives of people who had died and left money which hadn't
been claimed. On the Linkletter show they had named her
father, Chester Charles Hanson, and said there was an estate
that could total $200,000.

"I can't believe it!" Mrs. Gearin cried. "Where would he
get the money? He always said he had no money. I never
thought he had a cent."

But soon the truth of the story was established beyond
any doubt, when someone on the television show contacted
her and explained the details. Later a limousine arrived for
her and she appeared on a segment of Linkletter's program.
Then lawyers were engaged. After that began a period of
waiting.

For a time, the waiting drew the family closer together
than they had ever been. They still had no money, but
everyone participated in the game of planning for the day the

money would arrive, when a whole new life for them all
would begin. Lawyers haggled over their fees, over taxes, and
over disputed claims against the estate. For almost two years
the Gearins waited.

Finally, one Friday, the money arrived: a check for only
slightly less than $200,000. She didn't waste time staring at it.
Jolene had no sooner put the money in a bank than she began
to spend it. "The first thing I did was go out and buy myself a
little gold watch," she recalled later. "I'd always wanted one.
Then I found a beautiful sports car and paid $4,000 for it. I
just wrote a check, the first of many, many.

"I started to do everything I wanted to do. I just broke
loose."

Jolene and her children soon celebrated by going off on
a vacation together, just driving wherever they wanted. She
would drive her sports car a hundred miles an hour through
the desert, exhilarated by the feeling of speed. Then she'd
park the car and catch a plane, scattering travelers' checks all
over the country. Returning to Long Beach, she bought a new
home with four bedrooms and three baths, and filled it with
new furniture. It was a two-story house with plenty of room,
so all the kids moved in. Her husband, before long, returned.

An orgy of spending was justified, in Mrs. Gearin's
mind. "This was a positive thing," she said. "We decided we
were going to do all the things we always wanted to do but
never could afford."

They bought cars, trucks, motorcycles, clothes, a $2,000
hi-fi component system. Mother and daughters all had their
teeth capped. Mrs. Gearin had her breasts lifted. They all
began seeing psychiatrists. They flew to Australia. They in-
vested in the stock market.

When her youngest son, who was fifteen years old, said
he was interested in electronics, Mrs. Gearin bought him
$4,000 worth of equipment.

One daughter said she'd like to go to college, so Mother
laid out $6,000. The daughter rented a nice apartment,

bought furniture, enrolled in school, and began throwing parties.

One afternoon, one son said he'd like a motorcycle, so she took him to a store and bought the one he chose. He got on it immediately and sped away, enjoying it so much he rode until four o'clock the next morning, when he returned home and collapsed, exhausted on the floor.

One daughter wanted clothes and jewelry. "Go ahead and get them," her mother said without a second thought, and she hardly looked at the bills when she paid them. "We were wearing ourselves out spending," said Mrs. Gearin. "We were having a ball."

They bought ski equipment, appliances, and trinkets. People smiled at the way they always paid for everything in full, and the whole family was having the time of its life. Mrs. Gearin tried to spread it out evenly. "We need this spree," they told each other. "This is our extradition from slavery." A whole new world was indeed opening up to them, a world they had always been too impoverished to join.

Meanwhile, relations between Mrs. Gearin and her husband became increasingly strained. When he again went away, she began to accept the truth that she must have always known but had previously denied to herself: it wasn't the need for work and money that was keeping them apart; it never was. While she stayed home and tended the family, he had been free of obvious obligations as he traveled, and there must be other women. Mrs. Gearin made a decision she never would have dared before:

"One day I just said to myself, 'I'm tired of traveling all the time with a girlfriend or with the kids. I'm going to get myself a boyfriend.' Across the street lived a man whose girlfriend had just left him. I marched over there and knocked on the door. And for three months I had a torrid love affair, until it burned itself out. It was good to have the experience. I found that it wasn't what I wanted, it wasn't the kind of love I need, but I was glad to get it out of my system."

Soon she filed for divorce, deciding to live a life of her own rather than waiting for the occasional visits of a husband who really lived elsewhere. It astounded her to be awarded $10,000 in community property she hadn't known existed, and the court also ordered that she be paid $400 a month alimony, a sum that earned the reaction of a hasty shrug. She had grown accustomed to spending that much on a weekend.

More than a year had passed since the inheritance had arrived. It was closer to two years, she realized, and even her youngest child now insisted on leaving the nest to set up his own housekeeping. For the first time in her life, Jolene Gearin was completely on her own. If she wanted to lead her own life, she certainly had no reason not to.

One day soon after, a curt note arrived in the mail. It was from her bank, officially notifying her that her checking account was overdrawn. At first she tried to dismiss the matter from her mind; there must be some mistake. But a frantic telephone call verified the truth. The money was gone, all of it, in two years. Once again, she was broke.

Everything now began closing in on her. She felt pressure from all sides. The family started fighting among one another. They kept saying: "Why didn't we spend it this way?" "Why did you spend it that way?" Everyone seemed to blame her, and she could only protest: "You were all in on the spending. While the money was here, we all pitched in on that."

There were recriminations daily. Nobody felt they had gotten their fair share of the vanished fortune. Nobody could account for where it went. People were beginning to demand money they said they were owed. The house had to go; she couldn't keep up the payments anymore. And without the house, she didn't need the furniture, so some of it was sold for living expenses and the rest was just given away. The car had to be sold, too.

The worst was yet to come. When she was forced to move to a rented house in a lower-class suburb of San Pedro, word of her plight reached the local newspaper. She candidly confirmed the story and soon it appeared in newspapers everywhere that she had squandered a fortune in less than two years. The public reacted with the horror and revulsion usually reserved for those guilty of high crimes and misdemeanors. When the hate mail began to arrive, Mrs. Gearin already felt estranged from her children and other relatives. She felt her friends had deserted her, too. Now, letters from strangers were calling her the vilest of creatures and damning her for spending so much money so recklessly. People called her trash and said they hoped she lived in misery the rest of her days.

Mrs. Gearin blamed herself, too. "All right, I was not good at handling money," she told herself repeatedly, "but I never *had* handled money. I was completely unprepared for what happened."

Wherever she went now around the harbor city, she sensed resentment and ridicule. It was too much, she thought. Somehow she had to flee. What could be worse than the life she was living there? How could she possibly sink lower?

But there was a lower point she was yet to experience. To scrape together the fare to Australia, where one of her sons had moved at her expense, Jolene Gearin cashed in the last of what she owned. Carrying a mere 40 pounds of luggage, she fled the country, to escape what she felt were thousands of accusing fingers pointed at her. Months later, she was alone in the most remote northern coastal area of Australia, near Darwin, living in a tent, the only shelter she could afford. She felt like an outcast of society. She was down and out. Her son had wandered away to lead his own life with other young people.

"It was beginning to hit me, what an outcast I was," she related. "I was feeling very down one day, a feeling so low I couldn't bear it anymore. I'd never felt so low in my life. I just wandered along a cliff down to the beach. I remember sitting there for a long time with tears in my eyes, thinking that maybe this was the day to end it all. I just felt I couldn't go on."

Then, out of nowhere, she heard a voice, and turned to see a hippie youth standing before her. Many hippie groups had formed in that wilderness area where there was no one to bother them. She realized that several of them, boys and girls, had approached while she wasn't looking.

One stepped closer and asked, "Would you like a cup of tea?"

"Yes," she replied.

"Would you like to come to our tent for it?"

"No," she said.

He got a cup of tea and brought it to her. Even though it was a hot afternoon, the beverage was refreshing. As she sat there drinking it, several of the youths gathered around making idle conversation. Two of them had guitars and began to play, chatting with her between songs. They stayed for more than an hour and gradually her spirits rose. As she was returning to her tent later, she walked the miles slowly and thoughtfully, grateful for her acceptance by these people who, like herself, were outcasts of society. "I have them to thank," she realized, "or else I might have committed suicide."

She took up residence with the group and stayed on for two years. It was an easy life, subsisting on health foods and tea and the plentiful sunshine and water. In time, she began to reexamine what had happened to her back in Long Beach.

The inheritance had changed them all, she decided, and not really for the worst. The possessions were all gone, but something else remained. The son for whom she had bought electronic gear had gone into that business, something he never would have done without the money. Another son had had some scrapes with the law, minor things that teenagers often get involved in, and he might have wound up in jail without the legal help the money afforded. The daughter who had thought she wanted to go to college quit when given the chance, but she finally found her way of life in marriage. Another daughter, after conquering her feelings of inferiority, married a man with quite a bit of money; she had decided what she wanted and gone after it. So a lot of positive things had happened to the family that probably never would have happened without the money, Mrs. Gearin recognized in the aftermath.

As for herself, she had always thought that world travel would be the greatest possible life, and now, still friends with her divorced husband, she managed to travel more on her $400 a month alimony than she ever did on her inheritance. In fact, she learned how to handle money so well that she saved several thousand dollars over a few years, using it to journey from Australia to New Guinea, Hong Kong, India, South America, Central America, and Mexico. After five years she returned to Southern California to visit the children and her friends; she planned to move on to Oregon for a time and, when she had saved enough money, her next destination would be Africa.

Looking back on her life, she said, "When I had the money, I never left the country; and now that I do travel, I never tell anybody about my windfall, except that once in a while when I meet someone who really wants something badly, I say to myself, 'Gee, if I still had my money, I'd buy it for you, just like that.'

"When the money came was when I really started to see things. I think I've learned and grown spiritually, and I've had a lot of great experiences. Maybe after Africa I'd like to get married again, but the last thing I'd look for in a man is wealth, because I know how unimportant it is.

"But on the other hand, if it had never happened to me—the money—I'd probably still be sitting there looking out my window in Long Beach and hoping some day I'd be able to buy a new rug."

As Oscar Wilde once said, there are two great tragedies in life: not getting what you want, and getting it.

A young lawyer who had grown up in a well-to-do, re-spected family started gambling one weekend in Las Vegas. It was a case of beginner's luck: he won $13,000. Over the next

year he returned to the Gambling Capital often, losing a
couple of thousand every time. "Oh, well, it's not *my* money,"
he philosophized. He was $13,000 ahead, he figured, so in
theory he was still playing with the casino's money, not his
own. But soon he was $20,000 into his own money, throwing
away a small fortune in the attempt to recapture the glory of
the winning streak.

He blew it, as they say. But it's not unusual, psychoanalysts say, for people to repeat acts of extravagance, seeking to recapture the elation of their big win. People who
suddenly acquire money often suffer a wave of anxiety when
they find that their personal problems have not disappeared
as a result of their new wealth. Rather than face those problems directly, they seek the release of thrills and pleasure and
often end up flinging away their fortunes.

A rich, young commodities broker in Chicago, known
for his shrewd handling of funds in a field which, with its
huge winnings and losses, is not too far from gambling, commented: "People in my business have a tendency to self-
destruct. I think it's far more important to know what Freud
thinks about death wishes than what Milton Friedman thinks
about deficit spending."

The original name of the California city now called Ventura,
50 miles north of Los Angeles, was "Buenaventura," or good
fortune. Its sandy white beaches rise to lush green slopes that
afford a view of the spectacular Channel Islands offshore in
the Pacific. Once proud to call itself the Lemon Capital of
America, because of its extensive citrus groves, the city has
seen the orchards dwindle with the encroachment of oil drill-
ers and refiners with their malodorous tanks and dirty
equipment. In the part of the city most wasted by the oil
interests—the Ventura Avenue section—lived one Danny
Diaz, a 34-year-old house painter and odd-job worker.

Diaz, short and pudgy with straight black hair and a
poor complexion, tended to walk in a slouch, but he had

nevertheless a happy-go-lucky attitude toward life that quickly won over most of the people he met. He always wore jeans and a black fake leather jacket, and as for money, he rarely gave it much thought beyond calculating how many beers his few dollars would buy. But nobody ever called Danny Diaz stingy. He was known as a friend who'd buy you a beer with the last dollar he had.

Like dozens of others on his street, Diaz shared a rented bedroom in a small, boxlike stucco house set back from the sidewalk by a token, grubby lawn. Its doorway had a small portico above with a few red clay shingles as a token concession to architecture. Down the corner was one of the several taverns in the area where oil roustabouts hung around in their off hours.

It was the beginning of the week in late October 1975, and Danny Diaz had a job. A real estate company had hired him to repaint several old houses it had purchased for resale in Ventura County. Diaz got into his green 1966 two-door Buick and began the 25-mile drive to Sherwood Lake, a resort area just north of the Los Angeles County line. He had no reason to suspect that this day might be different from any other. The best he hoped for was a hard day's work and enough pay to contribute toward his rent and food. If it went well, maybe he'd treat himself to a beer or two after the job was done.

The drive took him past the ocean, through sweltering flat farmlands where strawberries and alfalfa are grown, up a steep five-mile grade into the Conejo Valley and then into hills forested with stunted oaks. There, with some difficulty, he located the address that he had been given, 714 Potrero Road. It was a big, old house fallen into disrepair but one that had been constructed by craftsmen who had used the best of materials. Diaz didn't know it, but the former tenant of the house, Elsie Canterbury, had died in the 1960's at the age of 77 and left an estate worth more than a million dollars, long since divided by heirs. The house had been sold as part of the estate.

It grew hot in the afternoon and Diaz, painting in a stuffy bedroom, opened the windows to let out the smell of paint while he tackled the hardest part of the room, the poorly lit closet. Like most closets, this one had received less cleaning through the years than the rest of the room. As he began rolling paint on the closet wall, Diaz felt a slight give under his feet, an unevenness in the floor. He stooped to look, running his fingers across the dusty but well-varnished boards. Strangely, the floorboards looked as though someone had cut out a square two feet wide and then replaced it. Why would anyone do that, Diaz wondered, in a house so well constructed? Usually, he knew, such trap doors were built only for access to wiring or plumbing, but in a closet floor?

Getting his putty knife, he pried up an edge of the boards; the whole little section lifted right out, and he set it aside. Then his heart began to beat faster. Sitting there in a perfect fit between the floor joists was a green metal box with a small silver handle. Diaz gently raised the box out and set it on the floor. It was locked. He tried, but could not open it. He knew there must be something of value in it, perhaps jewelry. He shook it, but there was no noise or shifting of loose objects. From the weight, he could tell it was full of something. He looked around, even though he was sure no one else was there. He was alone in the house. Nobody living knew of the box. Who would know if he took it?

He carried the small green box to his car, hiding it under some of his gear. Then he returned to his painting.

When he reached home late that day, Diaz leaped the three concrete steps to his doorway and raced for the privacy of his bedroom. He put the metal box on the bed, found a screwdriver, and desperately pried at the lock until it snapped open. He lifted the lid slowly, and his mouth fell open. The box was crammed full with money, bundles of it. He started grabbing them, but an instant later he stepped back, bewildered and disappointed. There was something wrong with the money. It looked more like *play* money.

The bundles of twenty-dollar bills, bound together with

paper clips and dried and cracked rubber bands, had a strange yellowish-orange tint that did not resemble real money. He looked closer. Maybe it was just faded with age. On the very top was a small piece of paper, three by five inches, with the figure, "$50,000."

It's got to be real, Diaz told himself, studying one of the bills carefully. It looked official. "The United States Will Pay to the Bearer Upon Demand Twenty Dollars in Gold," it said, and the bill was dated 1931. It felt like real money, too. And, he discovered, all the bills had different serial numbers. Some were labeled Silver Certificate. So it *was* real money, he decided, it was just old. Fifty thousand dollars! It was more money than he'd ever dreamed of having.

But he still wasn't sure. He held one of the bills up to the light that came from a window at the driveway side of the house. It sure looked real. There was only one way to be sure. Thrusting a handful of bills into his pocket, he closed the metal box, put it under the bed, and headed for a small tavern where most of the patrons were Mexican-Americans and where Danny Diaz was well known.

"Hey, this is real money, no?" he asked the bartender. The bartender consulted with another man, and Diaz worried. They examined the bill very closely, then told Diaz it was all right. Danny, relieved, had a drink then bought a round of drinks for the house.

For the first time since finding the metal box, Diaz began to relax. He had feared that when he showed the bill, the bartender would call the manager and the manager might call the police—despite the usual Chicano reluctance about doing so. But no, it was all right. He was rich. Danny Diaz was rich! All he had to do was keep his mouth shut and nobody would ever know where the money came from. Fifty thousand dollars! His mind raced. He began to make plans. What should he do? He could do anything he wanted. He ordered another drink. "Hey, bartender, a round of drinks for everyone."

He should, he thought, go back to work tomorrow as if

nothing had happened. He should call his relatives up north and tell them about it. Maybe he should go up there himself. He should change all the old money into newer bills that wouldn't attract attention every time he showed one. Sooner or later people would ask questions. He should not go to work tomorrow, he thought.

As the evening progressed, things became blurred. At some point he telephoned his relatives. He was feeling very generous at the bar, and the word quickly spread that Danny Diaz was buying drinks. Soon all of his friends were gathered around, and before long he had run out of money and had to go back for more. Back at the house—was it that night or the next day?—he told the man who lived in the house about the money, also the woman who lived there. And their three teenaged children soon knew about it too.

Some time in the next few days, a cousin or brother arrived and Danny Diaz remembered taking out $10,000, counting it off, putting it in a paper bag and then in the bureau drawer. Minutes later it wasn't there. Had he taken it to a bar? Perhaps. But other bundles of the money seemed to be gone, too. He didn't really care. He was very happy and not very sober, and his trips to the treasure box seemed not to seriously deplete the supply. He wasn't thinking very clearly. The celebration continued.

Several days later at a nearby high school, a teenaged girl waited nervously after the class bell rang. She wanted to see the teacher. She didn't know who else to talk to, and she felt she had to talk to someone. She stood in front of the teacher's desk and he asked what she wanted. "Is this real?" she asked, putting a yellowish twenty-dollar bill in front of him and trying to sound disinterested. "My mother said it was real, but I think it's counterfeit."

The teacher examined the bill and explained to her that, yes, the money was real, but it was a gold certificate, probably worth ten times as much as the twenty-dollar face value—not to be taken out and spent like just any twenty-dollar bill. Where did she get it?

Opening her purse, she spilled out a thousand dollars worth of bills from Danny Diaz's green box. She told the teacher that a man who lived in her house had a lot of money and that she was afraid her mother would get into trouble because of it.

"Maybe the police should know about this," the teacher suggested. "What if the money was stolen? If it was stolen, then it will mean trouble to anyone who touches it, no matter how genuine it is." Thus began the end of Danny Diaz's short, happy era of prosperity.

On the fourth morning after his windfall, Diaz awoke with a hangover. There was a roar and a shouting and the crash of metal against metal, and he saw before him the bars of a cell. He was sleeping on a thin mattress on a hard, red concrete floor in the Ventura jail. Instinctively, he thrust his hands into his pockets. Empty. He could have cried.

The noise and the shouting had been the rolling of the metal door and an officer calling his name. He was wanted for questioning. The police had gone to his room and found the box, which still contained $39,000. They had added the money he was still carrying when arrested, down to the last dime. The total: $39,453.10. Now the police wanted to know: Where was the other $10,000?

He didn't know, he told them. He didn't remember. Maybe he spent it or gave it away. But they already knew about the Canterbury house where he'd found it and that $10,000 had been put in a paper bag and taken away. Danny wondered if he himself had told the police that, or if someone else had told.

It didn't matter now though. Nothing mattered. His money was gone. It was all over. If only he'd kept quiet. If only he'd left town and not told anybody.

Two years later, the money that nobody had known about except Danny Diaz rested in a safety deposit box in a Ventura bank while several parties disputed its rightful ownership. An heir of Mrs. Canterbury, the trustee of her estate, and the people who had bought the house had all registered claims. Diaz, who had found the money, left town when they placed him on probation. He also entered a formal claim for the money, but he didn't really expect anything to come of it. After all, he had never had any luck.

Carly Mary Cady made an ideal contestant for the television game show. In her early thirties, she was slender in her green gabardine pant suit and short-sleeved silk blouse. Her hair was long and wavy, blondish-brown, and she wore blue eye shadow. She was attractive in a studied way, but not so glamorous as to inspire jealousy—in short, a woman with whom housewives would easily identify and for whom they would root to win.

The program was the now-defunct network game show "Now You See It," and by April Fool's Day, 1975, Carly had prevailed as the defending champion through eight shows. Now, if she answered one last question correctly, she would "break the bank" for a grand total of $19,000. She was sure the question would be a tough one. During a commercial break she gulped two Valium pills to suppress her nerves, though she knew winning contestants were expected to act hysterically. Drums rolled, the tension mounted, and at last the final question was posed: "Who was Popeye's hamburger-eating friend?"

"Wimpy!" she replied without a moment's hesitation. Then, remembering her coaching and knowing what was expected of her, she became the image of "a stark, raving maniac," screaming, jumping up and down, and throwing her hands to her head. Her hamming continued as she grabbed the master of ceremonies and accidentally bumped her head against his face. Thinking her hysterical laughter was crying, the emcee gave her a handkerchief as he nursed his own sore nose.

The show was over. She went to bed and slept for fourteen hours, then talked with her accountant, determined to put her winnings to sensible use. Her family had been well off

when she was a child, but her father died. When she left home
at 19, she had to work for a living, so she knew the value of a
dollar. She had worked her way through college as a secretary, telephone operator, and film production assistant.

The day after the show she took some friends out for
dinner to celebrate, and everyone was asking the same question: "What are you going to do with the money?"

Nineteen thousand dollars. Actually it was less because
$800 of it was in prizes, and the Internal Revenue Service
wanted $4,200 off the top. But $14,000, cash, is still a lot of
money.

"Put it in a savings and loan," her mother advised, "and
when you're sixty-five you'll have a million dollars."

Her doctor suggested Puerto Rican telephone bonds, 6
percent and tax free. What she really wanted to do was to live
for a year in Paris, but she worried about leaving because of
her mother's poor health. Maybe, she thought, she'd put a
down payment on a house. That would be a great investment.
She started looking at houses, meanwhile spending a little on:

A new wardrobe	$600
New typewriter	850
Recover couch	450
Two new chairs	550
Dermatology	85
Aquarium	50
Total	$ 2,585
Balance	$11,415

She paid off the balance owed on her car, paid a dental
bill for two new caps, spent a weekend in Las Vegas, moved
into a slightly more expensive apartment, and hired a twice-
a-month cleaning lady. She bought a lamp and a bookshelf,
spent about $400 on books, had her hair done a few times,
and her nails. And, oh, yes, three or four good-sized dinner
parties.

"Okay, but that still leaves me with $8,000," she noted after several months had passed. She couldn't find a house within her price range.

"Put the money in a savings and loan," her mother urged.

Miss Cady took her mother to Disneyland, and they stayed for two nights in a nearby hotel. She visited Palm Springs, gave a surprise party for eight at a nice restaurant. "Another time," she recalled, "I rented a limousine to pick up my date just to go to the movies—one of the hundred or so movies, plays, and operas that I attended during my spree." At Christmas, she sent out cards to all her cat's animal friends. She laughingly, and not inappropriately, called herself "Carly the Big Spender."

When she'd bought the expensive typewriter, she had intended to make a living as a freelance writer, and she did in fact manage to sell a few stories. But after a year passed she had to confess, "When it came to working last year, I didn't exactly knock myself out at the typewriter."

She was coasting, she knew, but she told herself, "What the heck, I didn't exactly break my back earning the money." When fifteen months had slipped by she reviewed her checkbook stubs and discovered that somehow, mysteriously, she was flat broke. She totaled it all up and sighed: "Unfortunately, day-to-day living expenses add up, so when all is said and done, the mystery isn't so mysterious anymore."

In need of a regular paycheck, she went back to work as a secretary and film production assistant at Paramount Studios. Occasionally she thinks about how the money just drifted away without one single major expenditure. No house. No Paris. Nothing in the savings and loan. But she's philosophical about it:

"It was a nice little windfall that made life a little better for over a year. It wasn't a large enough sum of money to overwhelm me, but it wasn't small enough to just throw away, either. The biggest mistake I made was just letting myself coast. Instead of using it as a nest egg, I took it too lightly, and now it's all gone. I wish I had been more observant and not just let it slip away without realizing what was happening.

"On the other hand, so what if I can't dip into my savings to pay the rent? It was great while it lasted."

Carly Mary Cady's, fortune, was only a small one, but what working person wouldn't love to have even $10,000 as a bulwark against the future's stormy financial seas? In Southern California, that sum invested in real estate would be as sure as rabbits to double in the briefest of time. On the other hand, Carly had displayed a distinct flair for acting rich, a trait which one day might attain riches for her if birds of a feather really flock together, or, if not, at least make the way a little brighter.

All over the world, fortune seekers are hunting for their pots of gold, swearing by all that's holy that they would not under any circumstances ever let a treasure, once landed, escape from their grasp. But who, of us can say for sure that we wouldn't, until we've met the chance?

It's ironic, in view of the widespread hunger for money, to consider the fortunes that sometimes seem to be everywhere, just waiting to be taken.

In a large eastern city as an armored truck pulled away from a curb, its rear door yawned open, and out spilled a canvas sack which immediately split open in the traffic and sent twirling through the downtown drafts a cascade of large bills. Most of the money was recovered from honest people, but others walked off with thousands. In Bethlehem, Pennsylvania, police were trying to find out who was flushing hundred-dollar bills down the toilet after recovering more than $4,000 from the sewer system. In Lovelock, Nevada, where bulldozers were carving out a new highway, there was discovered under an old wooden frame shack, long since abandoned by a Chinese resident, a cache of more than a hundred gold coins worth more than $27,000. It had been sitting there for 66 years.

Those three incidents occurred within one month in 1977.

Nobody knows how many years that $50,000 discovered by house painter Danny Diaz had remained hidden, but when the story came out, scores of treasure hunters invaded the area of the old house, figuring more money might be there. Guards had to be posted.

Some people don't even have to look. In St. Paul, Minnesota, an unemployed construction worker, Joseph G. Pearson, 52 years old, found in his mailbox a small fortune in checks: $25,000 in all. He partied, he vacationed, he bought things for himself and his family. He went to ball games and taverns, setting up drinks for the whole bar. The money went quickly, and when the state—which had sent him the checks through a computer error—came to get the money back, he shrugged. He thought the money had come in payment of a claim from a job injury that had kept him from working. Nothing could be done to get it back.

But whatever the source, fortunes large and small can appear suddenly anywhere, and can vanish just as quickly.

It was late July 1952 when Charlie "Hard Luck" Steen reached the lowest point in his 32-year life, a life already beset by enough misfortune to discourage any man. Thin and balding, but with wiry strength and determination, he stood alone on a sun-baked plateau in eastern Utah, near the Colorado state line, a ragged, fiercely independent prospector, his work clothes and open-top miner's boots stained with the red earth of that desolate area. He cursed to himself. The borrowed drill rig he was operating had just broken down a few feet short of his intended goal. Nothing was working out. Nothing was going right. It was almost ridiculous. Here he was, prospecting for uranium and too poor to afford even the basic Geiger counter.

He had started out over a year before with a trailer to

house himself and his wife, Minnie Lee, and their three children. Then she got pregnant and the fourth child came. There wasn't even enough money to buy milk, so they had to feed the infant tea instead. The trailer had to be sold for living expenses, but they found a tarpaper shack in Cisco, Utah, behind a gas station; it actually was the shell of an abandoned railroad freight car, without running water or toilet, and they rented it for fifteen dollars a month. The kids hadn't had a decent meal in months, and Steen owed everybody.

Most galling of all, though, to Charlie Steen, was the fact that people didn't take him seriously. He was always talking, always borrowing, always giving them his hard-luck stories and telling them that this time for sure, he was hot on the track of a million-dollar strike.

Though he was best known as a carpenter and odd-jobs man in the area, Steen had a geology degree from the El Paso (Texas) School of Mines, had apprenticed in the Peruvian jungles searching for oil, and knew as much as anybody else about the newly precious uranium. Still, it took a dollar to file a twenty-acre mining claim in the sparsely populated area, and he was finding it harder and harder to borrow a dollar these days. Despite his insistent optimism, he knew people considered him a loser, a loudmouth, a nut, who was accepted because prospecting always attracted a lot of odd people anyway.

The problem of the broken drill confronted him now, though. The expensive diamond bit, which belonged to a friend, had broken off short of the 200-foot level which he had decided he must reach, and there was no way to retrieve the bit with the equipment he had. To most people it would have been the last straw. He'd have to go back home again, with another hard-luck story, and try to borrow again.

His worn-out jeep stood nearby. Before getting in, he remembered the samples of strange, blue-black substance he had hit halfway down in the drilling process—too soon to be anything important, he thought, but material he couldn't readily identify. It was a long, dusty drive back, the 45 miles north to Cisco—a bitter drive.

Buddy Cowger, the gas station operator who was a part-time prospector, owned a Geiger counter, so when Charlie Steen pulled up, he decided to try the instrument on the unknown mineral samples before going back to face Minnie Lee. As Steen ran the prong of the Geiger counter over the samples, his heart jumped. The machine cackled wildly and the needle leaped immediately to the farthest point on the dial and never wavered. Then he knew. It was that rarest of all substances, pitchblende, the most concentrated form of uranium known to exist!

He whooped, he hollered, and he ran, gesturing wildly, shouting something about a million dollars and calling to Minnie Lee and the kids. Halfway there, Steen ran into a clothes line and knocked himself flat. But nothing could restrain his joy.

The strike, which was the first and biggest discovery of uranium in America in the newly born atomic age, eventually proved to be worth about $60 million.

For a long time, the celebrating never stopped. Steen ran wild. And why not? He felt he deserved it. He made no apologies for his money, declaring, "I didn't steal it, I didn't inherit it, and the only blood on it is my own."

His discovery was only the first of many as the area boomed, and Steen reigned for a time as the generous, uncrowned King of Moab, Utah, becoming popular enough to win election to the Utah State Senate.

As a spender, the new Charlie Steen was big. Even though he felt more comfortable in working men's clothes, he would stride into a haberdashery and order a dozen suits and shirts at a time. He decked his wife in expensive gowns, furs, and jewels. He'd spend $10,000 on a necklace as easily as some husbands buy flowers. Minnie Lee loved it.

He bought a 50-foot yacht and spent $150,000 getting it just the way he wanted it. Gradually, he acquired a fleet of private planes. But his crowning glory was yet to come. Upset at the rigid morality of the Mormon-dominated Utah, Steen moved to the green, forested Sierra slopes in northern Nevada, where he designed and built a spectacular palace costing $1.5 million. Its five domes were linked into a single roof like a circus tent and covered a sprawling 24,000 square feet; it was big enough for the average three-bedroom home, with landscaping, to fit in the living room. It had an indoor pool 40 feet long whose glass roof, at the push of a button, slid away to admit the heat of the sun.

Into this home he placed another million dollars in furnishings. He commissioned a huge mural depicting his uranium strike. A painting of the time he won $10,000 in a poker game with four aces. A sculpture of his mining boots. Minnie Lee's $25,000 Ming vase. Even the doors to his house, carved in red marble, cost enough to support the average family for a year.

The parties were endless. Especially the parties marking the July 27 anniversary of the big strike. He would send his planes to pick up guests. He had firm loyalties, and the old prospector who once had lent him a needed wrench was treated as royally as the banker who tended his fortune. "I used to get a kick out of mixing them," Steen said. "There'd be bankers standing next to scruffy prospectors. It was quite an assortment."

Said a friend who often attended Steen's parties: "They had as many as 8,000 people straggling in and out over a period of days in one single party. People would carry off twenty-pound pieces of barbecued meat and bottles of booze in the trunks of their cars."

Steen, who, when he traveled, carried around a briefcase full of hundred-dollar bills for expenses, commanded the treatment of a king and always got it. But he remained at heart a simple, shirt-sleeved fellow, always willing to talk to anyone, never pretentious. He enjoyed life, and didn't have a worry in the world.

After all, $60 million. Even if you never took it out of the bank, it would earn you $3 million a year in interest, which gives you over $8,000 per day for living expenses. You'd have to spend $400 an hour every waking hour just to exhaust the interest, and how could you do that without acquiring a lot of valuable assets?

In the early 1960's, Steen sold his lucky MiVida mine for $25 million, after a decade of prosperous ore sales. Advisors—he had a whole staff of them—had told him he must diversify. Others suggested he buy bonds and clip coupons the rest of his life, but that idea ran contrary to Steen's makeup.

He began diversifying. He bought a copper mine, a marble quarry, an aircraft factory, a cattle ranch, an orange orchard, even a pickle factory—thirty different companies in all. In his home, and in his office in nearby Reno, he welcomed ideas from anybody. It was an open door.

Things began to happen. A strike of smelters halted shipments out of his copper mine. Steen insisted on keeping his miners on full pay despite the shut-down; after all, it wasn't *their* fault. The aircraft factory suddenly was flung out of date by the introduction of the Lear jet. Beef prices fell below cost. His orange groves never produced. And even the pickle factory failed when the cucumber crop froze two years in a row. Flop, flop, flop. All around him it was happening. The marble quarry, promising $100 million worth of fine stone, proceeded nicely, but by 1967, when the enterprise still needed another six-figure sum to get its raw materials to market, Steen was in financial trouble.

Without warning, on February 28, 1968, agents of the Internal Revenue Service marched in and boarded up Steen's office while he was away, claiming that based on disputed deductions for past years, he owed them $2 million.

In its inimitably impersonal way, the government had turned on one of its biggest benefactors. Before Steen's discovery, the United States had had to buy its uranium from untaxable foreign sources such as Australia at more than five times the price it paid Steen per pound. In fifteen years he'd saved the government over a billion dollars and had paid millions in taxes, but now he was facing its cold, implacable stare, without even being granted an ear for his contention that he owed no such back taxes.

The IRS destroyed him, Steen said, by freezing him out. They tied up all his assets, stopped all his income-producing operations, and left him sitting penniless in his mansion for several years, while others to whom he owed money pressed for payment. One by one, his assets went on the auction block. His yacht was sold for $25,000, a fraction of its worth. His planes were seized and sold the same way, and everything else went piece by piece, for pennies on the dollar, until finally there was nothing left but bankruptcy and eviction from his 35-room mansion.

Steen went back to prospecting, prowling from the California desert to the Utah mountains, working out of Salt Lake City, determined to find another pot of gold. "I'm still better off than before I struck it rich," he said. "That's one good thing about this mess. I've gotten out from behind a desk and into the field, where I belong. And this time my four kids are all grown up and provided for, so I'm that much better off, ain't I?"

Undaunted, and willing to start all over in his fifties, Steen said: "I know I'll be wiser next time—about a lot of things. For one, I'll know who my friends really are. There are people I helped make millionaires who now act like they never heard of me."

Steen's son Mark added: "Yeah, remember _____? We knew him when he had holes in his carpet, but now he's too big to admit he knows us. I don't want to sound like a snob. I mean, there's nothing wrong with having holes in your carpet. But he forgets—"

Steen doesn't talk about *if* he strikes it rich again, but rather *when*. And he can be philosophical: "I knew the history of all the wildcatters in the West," he said, "I had read about all the other big plungers who got in too deep and spread their fortunes too thin, so I should have known better.

"Through the years I've seen and done everything a man can do with money, and nobody can ever take that away from me. If I've learned anything, it's that there's no such thing as financial security in this world. Opportunity yes, but no security."

"Windfall wealth is terrifying," the psychoanalyst Wahl commented. "In the mind, we treat such money as an ill-gotten gain, and the story has been repeated again and again in the lives of prospectors especially."

But whatever the source of a windfall, whatever its size—from five figures to countless millions—the whole thing can be blown away as swiftly as it came, leaving the mind reeling in disbelief and the suddenly-rich, suddenly-poor man uttering, "What happened?"

3. The Inheritance

Rosemary Jelneck's feisty little lapdog barked furiously as the two strangers appeared at the door of her country home, but Rosemary was expecting the men and invited them inside. They stood rather stiffly in their business suits as they introduced themselves and looked around the cozy, well-kept house. One of the men had called earlier, explaining that they wanted her help on a matter concerning the Security First Bank and Trust Company of Grand Haven, Michigan. When she agreed to see them, she expected only a brief interruption in the normal, busy routine of her day, that summer afternoon in 1966. Mrs. Jelneck, a small, brown-haired, 42-year-old housewife and mother of two teenage sons, had a full schedule caring for her family and working as part-time assistant to her husband Calvin, who ran his distributing business from an office in their two-story home in the small community of Swartz Creek, Michigan.

She ushered the two men into her living room, invited them to sit down, and settled herself into her favorite rocking chair. One man said he was an attorney and the other a trust officer for the bank.

"It's an estate matter," said the attorney. "We're looking for the next of kin of Arthur S. Kruse of Grand Haven. We thought you might help us."

"I've never heard of the man," Mrs. Jelneck responded without hesitation. "Who is he?"

"He *was* a retired insurance executive. He died suddenly while riding a bus in Pennsylvania. We thought he might be a relative of yours."

"Oh, no, I'm sure of that," she said. "My maiden name was Lindeboom."

A level-headed, easy-going woman, Mrs. Jelneck couldn't understand why these men had come all this way to see her. She repeated that she had never heard of Kruse and was certain he was not one of her relatives. In this rural area, everybody knew everybody else, and they certainly knew who their relatives were. Her parents were William and Mary Lindeboom. They were dead now, but they surely would have told her at some point in her life if she had a close relative named Arthur Kruse also living in Michigan.

She had grown up in Grand Rapids, living a perfectly normal, ordinary life. She had worked for a while as a secretary and had later married Calvin Jelneck. Several years ago, they had settled into small-town life in Swartz Creek, a community of 3,000 near Flint.

The family liked their quiet life in the country. Mrs. Jelneck enjoyed furnishing their home with comfortable early American furniture and found satisfaction in the homey pleasures of cooking and baking for her husband and two sons as well as making use of her secretarial skills in her husband's business. The one thing she really longed for was a house somewhere on a lake. She was a woman who appreciated the steady, comfortable course of her life.

That's why, as the reason for the visit of the two men

unfolded, it was like the opening of an incredible Pandora's Box, one that would not only change Mrs. Jelneck's future, but for the first time reveal to her the well-kept secret of her past.

The two visitors told Mrs. Jelneck that the late Arthur Kruse, who had recently died at the age of 67, had lived a modest, retiring bachelor life. He had had no children and had kept pretty much to himself. Kruse had devoted the last years of his life to fitting together the pieces of his family tree. He had, in fact, been stricken with a heart attack while riding a bus in Pennsylvania on his way to Detroit after visiting the New York City Public Library in the course of his genealogy research. He had left no will.

Two of Kruse's known cousins had gone to Grand Rapids to make burial arrangements and to ask Security First Bank and Trust Company to close what was presumed to be a modest estate. But bank investigations had uncovered surprise after surprise in accumulated wealth: He had left in all $1,688,000, most of it in stocks and the rest in bank balances, real estate, and personal property.

While the estate was being appraised, a bank official had turned up four more cousins who appeared to be among Kruse's next of kin. He had had a sister, Mrs. Ann Corbin, who had died just three years earlier. At a court hearing on the determination of legal heirs the six cousins had agreed that, to the best of their knowledge, they constituted all the known kin of the late insurance executive Arthur Kruse.

About this time, however, notebooks had surfaced which Kruse had filled with references to his family tree, including cryptic references to a lost niece, Eugenia. The notes suggested that Mr. Kruse's sister, Ann Mercedes Kruse Corbin, had had a daughter who, for reasons unspecified, had been placed in an orphanage in Grand Rapids.

A trust officer for the bank had immediately begun a search for more information about the child. He had tracked down a Grand Rapids record of the marriage of Ann M. Kruse to Earl R. Corbin on February 4, 1913. After searching through her effects he had found a letter dated May 19, 1925, which referred to a child Eugenia. The bank official had then checked the county birth records and discovered an entry which showed a female child had been born on August 16, 1924, to a woman giving the name Mercedes Kruse.

Like fitting together the pieces of an intricate puzzle, the trust officer had examined the records of the Catholic Social Services Organization and had found an entry which said that Eugenia, for unknown reasons, had been placed in St. John's Home, a Grand Rapids orphanage, on December 17, 1924. Just three days later she had been adopted by William and Mary Lindeboom.

The trust official had located a nephew of the late Mr. Lindeboom and confirmed from him that a baby girl had indeed been adopted and raised by the Lindebooms as their own. Eugenia Kruse had been renamed Rosemary Lindeboom. The couple had sworn all relatives to secrecy. They had even gone so far as to have a false birth certificate drawn up and to convince a city official to sign it so it would look as though Rosemary was their natural child.

The two bank representatives produced the incredible evidence and presented the documents to Mrs. Jelneck, proving beyond any doubt that she really was that adopted child, Eugenia. Understandably, she could not at first believe it and insisted that they must be mistaken. They had twisted her simple past into some strange unrecognizable shape. She felt that what they were saying just couldn't be true. As she ushered them out the door, she was still shaking her head in disbelief and wondering what her husband would think of this fantastic story.

Later, Mrs. Jelneck confronted a cousin and an uncle with the bizarre story. They denied it at first but finally admitted to her that it was all true. As she listened, it seemed her whole world was being pulled out from under her. She was more shocked to learn that she was an adopted child than that she was about to inherit nearly $2 million.

Unanswered, probably forever, were the questions behind the known facts: What was the dark secret of 1924? Whatever happened to Eugenia's real father? Why was the child placed in an orphanage? Did the uncle know that Eugenia was Rosemary? What circumstances made the uncle—who as an insurance executive knew the importance of a will—leave instead a trail of family tree notes which the estate administrators said seemed designed to lead to Eugenia?

On October 7, following a 40-minute hearing in the Ottawa County Probate Court, a judge ruled that the Swartz Creek housewife was the sole heir of the entire estate of Arthur S. Kruse. Mrs. Jelneck left the courtroom still shaken, but happy with her tremendous fortune. It meant the realization of one of her fondest dreams: not the money, but a tri-level house on a lake that was part of the Kruse estate. It was something she'd always wanted, and before long she and her family moved in.

Aside from the longed-for lakeside home, the dropping of a fortune into their midst cast hardly a ripple through the Jelneck family. They went along much as before, except for going out to dinner more often. Jewels, beautiful clothes, cars, and the like were things Mrs. Jelneck neither needed nor desired. She didn't even hire outside help with the housework: she'd always done it herself and that's how she wanted it now.

Just five years after becoming a millionaire, Mrs. Jelneck died of cancer in a hospital in Grand Haven. The money was divided equally among her husband and two sons. Twenty-nine-year-old Thomas, married, with three children, moved to Connecticut. Twenty-five-year-old Donald stayed nearby in Michigan with his wife. And Calvin Jelneck remained in the tri-level house in Spring Lake.

Donald, despite all his money, worked at jobs during his college years, ranging from mixing cement to meat cutting. Armed with a degree in business administration, he then joined his brother and father in their plans to open a clinic for alcoholics.

"It's nice to have the money for the security it gives you," Donald Jelneck said. "I could have bought a $100,000 house, but I bought a modest one, because fancy houses aren't important to me. I've always worked and I always will, because a person has to be busy in life. Right now I'm mainly interested that the clinic runs smoothly. I guess I don't worship money. That's the way my mother was, too."

The fascination of lost heirs has attracted widespread interest through the years, as a result of the fact that an estimated $20 billion in bank accounts, stock certificates, and other property lies unclaimed in bank vaults and other legal depositaries around the world, most of it destined to revert to state ownership if the rightful heirs cannot be located.

One Manhattan-based company, Missing Heirs International, claims to have found 80,000 heirs through the years, delivering to these astonished people sums ranging from a mere $1,000 to $7 million in estates they never knew existed, from relatives they'd never met.

In one case, the company located a California man employed as a middle-level business executive, informing him that he was the rightful heir to a $6 million bequest. All he had to do was go to court and admit that he had been an illegitimate child. The man refused. He liked his life the way it was. He did not wish to risk embarrassing people close to him by bringing up unpleasant facts about his origins.

The incidence of lost heirs has increased greatly in recent years, especially since World War II, when so many families were scattered by migration to distant parts of the country. But America has always been a place of separated families, many people tracing their ancestors to foreign lands where relatives still dwell, out of touch for decades and often forgotten.

Imagine the surprise of a 43-year-old female prisoner at the Orange County Jail in California, serving a one-year sentence for writing bad checks, when she was informed that she was the heir to a $4 million estate that had been left in the hands of a financial institution!

When Edwin Lewis Clark, at the age of 49, died unexpectedly in 1967 in a Veterans Hospital in Los Angeles, where he had been taken because he had service as a sergeant in the Air Force, it was assumed he was a pauper. The stocky, blue-eyed man had lived in the smog belt of downtown Los Angeles in a small, modest apartment in a building occupied mostly by older, retired people. He had only two suits to his name, and all his personal belongings, including a table radio and pots and pans, fit into two small cardboard boxes when they cleaned out his room. Receipts left in a drawer, however, led the County Administrator to a broker in Beverly Hills. The broker revealed that Clark had an investment portfolio that included stock in United Artists worth $3 million.

Further tracing was difficult because Clark had changed his name from Jasewicz sometime after leaving his family of three sisters and a brother in the 1930's and joining the military; he had served at Pearl Harbor during the attack, and had later traveled around the world as a "career man," putting in a total of twenty years before retiring in 1956. Finally, his relatives were located in Pennsylvania. They had seen him from time to time, but not in the twelve years since he left the Air Force.

One sister, Mrs. Jean Fogel of Philadelphia, told estate investigators that she had heard he had moved to Florida, got married and divorced over the years, and only recently had moved to California. No one had any idea he had any money other than his small military pension.

The $3 million estate was divided among three sisters in Philadelphia, and a brother Joseph, who had moved to Deerfield, Illinois.

"Mike's Place" was as old and time-worn as the word "saloon" itself. The dilapidated, white wood-frame building with its steep, tar-papered roof stood against a pine-covered cliff on a lonely roadside not far from Mount Shasta in Northern California. It looked more like an old-timer's jerry-built summer cottage than a place of business, unless you caught sight of its small Coca-Cola sign. Curiously, a brand-new, $40,000 Rolls Royce always sat parked in front.

Inside, where there was no mistaking the premises for anything but a saloon, the owner, Mike Padula, tended bar and occupied modest living quarters in back. A small, slow-moving man with wide-set eyes and a bald head, Padula seldom cracked a smile unless he was talking about the old days, which, since he'd been polishing his mahogany bar for a half century, meant the 1920's to him.

His customers generally came from the local area or had been told by friends that if they ever went to Northern California they should visit this relic from the past for nostalgia's sake. Everybody knew that Mike's Place was not a money maker. It was felt that lonely old Padula just kept it going so that there'd be some people around to talk to. He told them stories about the era of bootlegging when Mike's Place had been a prospering roadhouse. As a young man, he told those who would listen, he had dodged bullets, run with powerful people, and dated movie beauties.

Tourists gaped at the raunchy decor. Through the years a collection of girlie pictures—gas station calendars, Vargas and Petty girls from the early Esquire magazines—took over all four walls. Almost every other blank surface was scrawled in lipstick with girls' autographs. A small, superannuated heater with its single stovepipe running up through the roof, an ancient piano, and several covered game tables stood there, leftovers from the Twenties. The smell of cigarette smoke and stale beer had soaked into the very timbers.

Little was known about Padula and it was assumed that he had no family. He lived alone and nobody ever got very close to him. He had shown up in the hamlet of Castella, California, in 1919, and was hired as a busboy in one of the local hotels when the area was known as a summer resort featuring hot springs on the banks of the Sacramento River.

He told people he had been born in Italy and raised in
Marlboro, Massachusetts, and that he had served in World
War I. He never mentioned that he was one of a dozen
brothers and sisters in a family which had scattered through
the years. When he had returned from the war, he had found
his mother due to give birth to her twelfth child and had left
home before the blessed event, never contacting anyone in his
family again.

Once in the 1940's his youngest sister, the one who was
born after he left, sent a letter addressed, "Mike Padula, Castella, California," and enclosed photographs of her two infant
daughters, but he never answered her.

As the years passed, Padula earned a reputation as a sort
of character, part of the local color. He covered his bald head
with a Tyrolean hat sporting a multicolored feather, and he
drove expensive cars like the Rolls Royce, but vehicles were
his only apparent extravagance. It was rumored that he had
made some money in the Prohibition days and had salted it
away for his old age.

One chilly Saturday afternoon in November 1972,
Padula was returning from a drive to Mount Shasta where he
had gone grocery shopping. He got out of his silver Rolls,
clutched his chest, and fell dead of a heart attack. He was 77.
His will directed that he should lie in state in a shiny copper
casket inside Mike's Place, and that—short of being buried in
his Rolls Royce—his crypt should display a picture of the
vehicle imbedded perpetually in ceramic. But these were not
the biggest surprises. Padula left an estate that included $1.5
million in stock in a supermarket chain and about an equal
sum in property.

It may never be known what Padula felt about his family
or why he estranged himself from them. It's hard to believe
that in 50 years no other human came closer to his heart
through act of kindness or friendship. But whatever went
through the secret mind of the lonely old saloon-keeper, he
left his entire estate, worth approximately $3 million, to be
divided equally among the one sister he never saw and her

two daughters, whose pictures she had mailed to him.

When word reached Monroe, Michigan, on Lake Erie between Detroit and Toledo, Mrs. Pamela Gray, the sister, was working in the classified advertising department of the local newspaper. Her two daughters, married and in their mid-twenties, lived nearby. Notified of the inheritance by telephone, they were taken completely by surprise; it was a total shock.

"I couldn't believe it," said one of the daughters. "I only vaguely remembered that mother had said we had an uncle somewhere in California, and no one knew anything about him. No one ever thought he might have money." A short, attractive young woman with brown hair and hazel eyes, she said she was sorry that Mike Padula had died without ever being reunited with his family. She, her sister, and her mother, valuing their small-town lifestyle and determined that the inherited money will not radically alter things, shunned the attention that was focused on them as a result of the news of the unexpected bequest. But she admitted that, in idle hours when she knits and crochets, she often thinks about the uncle she never met.

He must have thought a lot about her.

Even though stories of heirs who run amok with their inheritance are noted from time to time in the press, the vast majority of estates, large and small, pass from parents to sons and daughters with no upheaval in their lifestyle, and that applies whether the bequest routinely transfers into the survivor's hands at an anticipated, appointed date such as the twenty-first birthday, or if it comes unexpectedly from a distant, unknown source.

"It comforts the nonrich to believe that money cannot buy happiness and that wealth and misery are inevitable companions," said George G. Kirstein in his book, *The Rich: Are They Different?*. But, he added, he had made a study of all the various indices of unhappiness such as suicide, drug addiction, and alcoholism and, allowing for the fact that the rich tend to attract more attention in the press, he concluded that if a rich man displays unhappiness with his money it probably stems not from the money but from unhappy childhood relationships, of the same kind as those that afflict the poor.

Those who handle their lives best when they receive a windfall large enough to change everything seem to be the same people who would handle their lives best even if they had never gotten such a fortune.

Sometimes word of a huge inheritance reaches a family and throws it into excitement and turmoil, but then, as claims and counterclaims move matters into the snail-like processes of the courts, the people are left hanging on and hoping for years, and their lives, as they await the outcome, are almost suspended.

Pending in the 1970's were numerous cases that could enrich individuals, entire families, even, in certain cases involving Alaskan natives and American Indians, entire tribes.

In 1966 the Peruvian-born Mrs. Raymond Verrill, who moved to Huntington Beach, California, in 1949, was informed by the Peruvian Embassy that she was one of eight descendants of Antonio Pastor De Marin, the Spanish Viceroy who ruled over Peru in the late 1700's. The Viceroy left a will designed to disinherit a son, specifying that his fortune be held for any fifth-generation descendants surviving in the twentieth century.

Officials of the Banco Commercial del Peru advised Mrs. Verrill that they were holding what appeared to be a valid receipt of deposit for the Viceroy's fortune, which had been placed in a foreign bank, the old Bank of Scotland, for safekeeping. The total sum: 460 million pounds sterling, which, at the going exchange rate, would have exceeded one billion dollars. A search began of all Scottish banks which had existed prior to 1800, but the vast hoard could not be found.

"We will wait and see," said a complacent Mrs. Verrill. "But I consider myself rich already. I have health and happiness."

In Prattsville, Arkansas, there is no traffic problem, no welfare problem, no crime problem, no drug problem, no smog
problem, and God is not dead. The two-lane highway
through Prattsville passes the store, the church, the gas station and garage, and all the other businesses in town, and if
you take a left or a right turn, you're in the residential area.
The homes are neat and well kept, and life centers around the
Harmony Baptist Church, all local residents being members.

For a dozen years, through a maze of courts all the way
up to the United States Supreme Court, tedious legal
technicalities had been argued with little public attention in a
case alleging that a small, partially submerged island in the
mouth of the Mississippi River, at Buras, Louisiana, had been
wrongfully occupied by oil companies who assumed they
could drill there under a long-standing off-shore rights
agreement.

On October 31, 1970, the authoritative, ever-watchful
New York Times was the first to report that a decision had been
reached in the case, with the Supreme Court ordering the oil
interests to pay the sum of $86.5 million to the Buras family,
which claimed ownership of the island. The report added that
the Mr. Buras who had filed the suit years before had become
totally disabled and had transferred his power of attorney to
his son, Jack Buras of Prattsville, Arkansas.

The world soon beat a path to Jack Buras's door, a
hundred miles north of Louisiana in the small Arkansas town,
population under 1,000, the kind of place where everybody
knows everybody else.

At the farthest edge of town sat an aluminum-sided
mobile home beside an untilled field. A wooden step led to
the metal door of the home where Jack Buras lived with his
wife Barbara, the daughter of a minister, and their daughter
Melody, age two. Buras, who stood six feet six inches tall, with
his weight well distributed, could be mistaken for a football
player because of his build but there was not an ounce of
menace in his entire body when he approached.

He was 23 years old and loved his job, teaching music to

the church's youth choirs, and running the youth activities programs despite the meager salary of just over a hundred dollars a week. It's not clear just how word of the multimillion-dollar award reached town, but it seemed that everybody knew about it immediately. Some said that the local paper from a nearby town had telephoned Buras but others said no, he'd had an official letter about it weeks before.

Presenting a classic picture of rural shyness, Buras initially acted almost embarrassed about the money and certainly by all the attention it had brought. "At first I didn't know what they were talking about," he said. "We were always poor. There was my brother, sister, mother and dad, and dad was always sick. I remember from the time I was a kid dad used to talk about how he was going to get rich because of some court case, but I never paid much attention to the details. Then, no sooner than it happened, he died. He was poor all his life and then he died and never lived to see the money."

Of course, Buras explained, even though he was named the principal heir, he would see that the money was divided among all the family members. "But I haven't received a cent yet," he said. "They told me the $86 million was in royalties kept in escrow all during the case, but they've still got to decide if they have to pay interest on the money, and then there's probate of Dad's estate. They said it could take years."

Nevertheless, the positive signs of riches began to flow without delay. A local automobile dealer rolled a new Thunderbird up to Buras's door and told him to keep it, pay for it some day if he wanted to, or just keep it. He loved the car, so he kept it. "I guess he knows what he's doing, because I'll probably buy dozens of cars from that dealer on account of this," Buras said, "but it made me feel funny, because if I had walked into his showroom, I couldn't have afforded even the down payment."

Banks all over the state seemed to be tripping over one another in an effort to be first to practically hand him the keys to their vault. He was extended an open line of credit at several banks and he swiftly formed a corporation of his own.

"These people are falling all over themselves to lend me as much money as they can," Buras said. "I suppose they heard that I plan to set up a million-dollar trust fund for my daughter, and another one for our second child which is on the way, and there aren't many trust funds that big in Arkansas banks.

"I suppose everybody's waiting for me to run wild," Buras said. "But I don't think it will happen." With some pride he declared, "Barbara's the level-headed one in the family. You know, we could build a $200,000 home with maids and chauffeurs and all that, but she said we can't.

"I wanted to do something special nice for her so I got her a Lincoln Continental, a beautiful two-tone car, but when she saw it she said, 'Jack, take it back. I can't drive that. What will our friends think? It would look like we were deliberately showing off.' So I took it back and told them I was sorry. I was going to get her a plain old station wagon instead, but I haven't got it yet, so she's still driving our old Volkswagen."

In the first few months after the news about his inheritance, Buras and his wife received 10,000 letters from all over the world, most of them asking for money. "We kept track of the money requests at first, until they reached $100 million. Then we stopped counting."

His wife added, "Then we started burning all the mail for a while, until Jack's friends complained he wasn't answering *their* letters."

The investment schemes were wild. A million-dollar bicycle shop in Manhattan. Reconstruction of an Australian pioneer village. "And somebody wanted me to finance a Christian race track, whatever that'd be."

"A lot of it is funny," Buras said, "but I don't want to become callous to people and their needs. There are some good ideas people have written me about and maybe I'll try one or two some day."

It was the flood of business propositions brought about by his instant fame that led Buras to form a corporation to

organize the enterprises he was interested in. Even if he
didn't get his inheritance for ten years, he commented, he'd
probably be rich by then as a result of his involvement in so
many ventures.

But as time went on, people began to remark that Buras
seemed to be under a strain. He acted disgruntled and the
ready smile he was known for now seldom appeared. About
the only time he really behaved like the old Jack Buras they
knew was when he was at church.

The Harmony Baptist Church, where he had continued
working as choir director, evokes thoughts of a picture post-
card of rural America, a gleamingly clean, simple structure
with steeple prodding the blue sky. In the warm interior, near
the altar, Buras rehearsed a dozen well-scrubbed youths from
nearby farms, practicing all the traditional hymns over and
over to such perfection that tears welled up in his eyes. He felt
comfortable among the kids. With them, the money was never
mentioned. They liked him, flocked around him not because
he was a prospective millionaire but because he was their
choir leader. He had gotten them on television once and he'd
had them record an album of songs.

Trying to explain his apparent discontent, Buras said:
"It's a little disappointing to suddenly become rich like I have.
It isn't at all the way you've always dreamed it would be. I wish
actually it had happened later, ten or fifteen years from now,
maybe when I was 35 and I'd had a chance to get my feet on
the ground.

"You see, I felt I was just getting started on the right
track with what I wanted for myself and my family. This is a
good life. This is just the groove I wanted to be in. I want my
kids to grow up here in a normal life, going to public schools
and maybe getting a bloody nose in a fight on the way home
just like I did. I hope I don't sound naive, like some kind of
nut, but this is a good life.

"You know, some days—I've had a lot of business
headaches connected with getting rich and some days I feel all

worn out before sundown. Then I go to church and start
rehearsing these beautiful kids in the choir and suddenly I'm
enjoying myself again."

With a trace of irritation he said, "I want to be something besides just a millionaire." He shrugged and added, "I
guess maybe one man out of ten thousand gets a chance like
this—to do something really worthwhile. Well, I don't want to
look back and see that I'd had my chance and missed it."

Not long after that, Buras and his entire family disappeared. There was no forwarding address. People who were
considered closest to them said they were mystified. Why had
they gone? Where had they gone? Everyone was asking: What
happened?

An area newspaper printed some strange reports.
Buras, they said, apparently was not an heir to an $86 million
fortune. The Buras oil family of Louisiana had been contacted and had stated that he was not known to be a member
of the family, not *the* Buras family.

People who knew Buras refused to believe that he was
not completely genuine. Despite the mysterious disappearance, one friend said incredulously, "Jack? Jack trying to pull
the wool over people's eyes? Never." He laughed and added,
"Jack had a heart as good as gold."

Many believed that if the whole thing had been a mistake of some kind, Jack Buras had been deceived, too. Maybe
the courts sent him some papers on the inheritance by mistake, it was reasoned, because his name was the same as
another Jack Buras, and he just accepted it. Or maybe people
just told him he was rich and he believed it.

Few people were ready to accept the possibility that the
well-liked Jack Buras and his sweet wife could have played
some kind of a deliberate hoax. It just didn't make sense. Not
the Jack Buras they knew.

A theory emerged. What really happened was, they said,
that the pressure finally got to him. All he wanted was the
simple life he had once had, and ever since the word got out
about his inheritance, people had been hounding him, for-

tune hunters of all types. Maybe some kook even threatened the family. Finally, he decided the only way to escape all the trouble was to disappear just the way he did and to make people think that it had never been real. Then he'd be left alone.

In the mid-1970's, Jack Buras reportedly was connected with a music publisher in Lousiana, a travel agency in Florida, and other pursuits in the South. But he remains submerged in mystery, as much so as the tidelands oil fortune remains buried in litigation.

There are some striking similarities between the Buras story and another one, which had its beginning and end less than 200 miles east of Prattsville, Arkansas.

In the late 1950's Ernest Medders was a husky, balding, middle-aged man with a small-town, folksy geniality. He and his short, plump wife Margaret eked out a living at the near-poverty level in Memphis, Tennessee, he as a sometime mechanic earning $75 a week and she employed as a nurse's aide in a local hospital.

When all the Medders kin were called to a special meeting in Centerville, Alabama, the Memphis couple scraped up the fare and went. They had been told it was important, and as it happened, it was the turning point of their lives.

A Mississippi lawyer stood in front of them waving some important-looking documents and citing chapter and verse about how Medders' father, and his father before him, settlers on the Texas range who had been ousted despite legitimate claims, were the legal and rightful heirs to the famous Spindletop oil fortune. The lawyer set forth his detailed plan for filing this claim in federal court, but Medders wanted to get down to brass tacks: How much did it mean in dollars?

"Five hundred million," replied the lawyer. And he must have had impressive papers to back up what he was saying, because Medders, who admitted he couldn't even read, upon returning to Memphis, immediately found himself able to borrow a seven-figure sum against the forthcoming inheritance. Why wait for the lawyers to iron out the details?

The Medders soon packed up and moved to a Texas ranch more befitting their new station in life. They bought two ranches, actually, the homestead being at Muenster, 60 miles north of Dallas, where they put up a house worth a quarter of a million dollars and a barn for $175,000. The smaller ranch, a mere three hundred and some acres, boasted eighteen producing oil wells. The ranch, which Medders called Colonial Acres Farms, was stocked with prize Angus cattle, including a stud valued at more than $100,000. Fancy Appaloosa horses, some costing more than $10,000, also were shipped in to begin one of the finest breeding operations in Texas.

Texas society soon was buzzing with news of the Medders family, whose members sped about the rural roads in two Cadillacs and a station wagon. They bought a townhouse in Dallas so they wouldn't have to stay in hotels during overnight visits, and they began spending at the rate of about fifteen or twenty thousand dollars a week. Parties at the ranch became the highlight of the Dallas social calendar, with 800 to 1,000 guests convening. People were flown in by tuxedo-clad pilots, or they rode private trains and special buses equipped with bar and a free-flowing champagne fountain. The hosts dressed in finery, furs, and jewelry from elegant stores like Nieman Marcus.

Soon their $50,000 parties and free-spending lifestyle—which one neighbor compared to that in Edna Ferber's *Giant*—were attracting the cream of Texas society. Congressmen, important local officials, even the state governor traipsed out to the Medders ranch. President Lyndon B. Johnson invited the Medders to the White House for dinner and flew them home in Air Force One.

By 1967 the Medders' credit was so firmly established that they were able to borrow another three-quarters of a million dollars from hard-nosed bankers who had not noticed that the United States Supreme Court in 1965, had quietly dismissed their claim to the Spindletop oil fortune as having no merit.

Later that year, an overdue $3,000 feed bill toppled the Medders empire. When the feed store owner pressed for payment, Medders admitted that he had never received a cent of his supposed inheritance and had in fact, been living for seven years on borrowed money. Aghast creditors formed a line all the way from Dallas to Colonial Acres Farms, which went on the auction block as the bill collectors settled for a few cents on the dollar, at best.

The Medders apologized for the multimillion-dollar misunderstanding. "We're just poor people who believed the lawyers when they said we'd inherit $500 million," they explained, "and when you believe that, you don't care how much you spend."

Just as quietly as they came, Ernest and Margaret Medders moved back near Memphis to live out their days on a Social Security check of about $260 a month, staying with a cousin across the state line at Horseshoe Lake, Arkansas.

Whatever the final outcome of the Buras and Medders stories, they serve, at least, to illustrate this truth about money: To be treated like a millionaire, and even to live like one, you don't necessarily have to have a dime to your name.

4. Marrying a Millionaire

In her small, dimly lit hotel room, Barbara Stewart, a blonde in her early thirties, made a final inspection of herself in the scratched dresser mirror, brushing her shiny, straight hair down to her shoulders and turning to examine her dress. She wasn't quite satisfied with the basic black dress she wore, coming as it did from the sale rack in a bargain department store, but it was neat and businesslike, without hiding her slim figure, and anyway it was the best she had.

Hurrying to an appointment, she hoped she could hide how desperate she really was. She prayed that the businessman she was scheduled to meet could and would help her. She decided not to tell him how she had acquired the stock shares she wanted to sell. That might be telling too much. The truth was, she was flat broke. She had been stuck in Casper, Wyoming, doing assay reports, recording deeds, and handling the paper work for a small, struggling mining company that was always promising to pay her "next week for sure."

Months had gone by without a paycheck and she had to work at the switchboard in her hotel and serve cocktails in the lounge at night to pay for her meals and the nine-by-twelve room. When the mining company finally went bankrupt, they had offered to settle with her the only way they could, with some leftover mining stock. And a name had been mentioned. "See Robert Crail," they had told her. "He might help you sell it."

She had heard about Crail. He had a reputation for putting together companies, for being a real wheeler-dealer who cruised around the mountains in a specially-built lavender Cadillac scouting for precious metals. But meeting Crail turned out to be different from what she had expected.

He was a short, dark, Lebanese businessman in his early forties, and his dynamic manner immediately fascinated her. Most of the men she'd met the last couple of years were what she called "professional dreamers." They went around leasing and exploring mining properties, always believing that the next day they would find their pot of gold. This man Crail had made his own fortune, but he still didn't treat her as if she and her little stock deal were unimportant. They found they enjoyed talking to one another and, after he had agreed to help her sell her stock for the several hundred dollars she so desperately needed, they sat in a coffee shop for hours.

Relieved by the solution of her cash problem, she soon found that she and Crail had quite a lot in common. Both had been born and raised in poverty, she in Yuma, Colorado, he in Asia Minor. His manner was so easy that she didn't feel she had to impress him.

"I was the oldest of twelve kids in a farm family," she told him, "and we were so poor I grew up fat from a diet of beans and potatoes. On Sunday we'd have chicken, and that was the only decent meal of the week. Usually we were all packed into two rooms, because my father was always buying a farm and losing it or selling out. We didn't even have electric lights until I was in my teens."

"My real name," he told her, "is Abraham Ayash, but I use the name Robert Crail for business in America. It sounds better."

He praised her dress and she told him that when she was a kid at school they used to call her "Rags" because her clothes were always old, out-of-style, second-hand things. It was hardly the stuff of romance. She even told him, directly contrary to her original intentions, the worst of her troubles. "I was married to an insurance executive," she said. "It was my second marriage. My first marriage, when I was a teenager, was to a guy I thought was rich. He was a truck driver, but compared to what I had known, a truck driver *was* rich. The marriage just didn't work out, though. The insurance executive, he took me to Wyoming on a business trip, and we left the four kids with my mother in Colorado. Then he disappeared. Just ran off and left me stranded in a hotel with no money to pay the bill and thousands of dollars worth of bouncing checks. So what was supposed to be a five-day trip to Casper stranded me for a year and a half just trying to pay off the bills."

Ayash told her tales of the business world he moved in, how *Life* magazine had once called him "a young King Midas" because everything he touched turned to gold, how he and his friends had once chartered an airliner and flown the whole chorus from a Las Vegas club to the Virgin Islands for a party. He talked about oil tankers in the Mediterranean and laughingly described how his head spun trying to juggle twenty different companies at once.

They had met at four o'clock for what was to have been a brief business session, but midnight passed and they were still talking. He promised to telephone her next day.

When he called, he asked her to dinner and took her to an Arabic restaurant. She enjoyed the spicy, exotic food, the warm lighting, the rich decor. Ayash, whose manner was strong and self-confident, suddenly announced, "You're going to be my woman."

"I'm no one's woman," she replied firmly. Even though she liked him, she'd just been through a disastrous marriage and she didn't feel ready for another serious relationship. All she wanted, she said, was to take the money from her stocks and get her kids back with her, to start life over again.

But Ayash persisted, and within a couple of weeks he returned to the subject, even getting down on his knees to say, "Will you marry me?"

Ten years later Barbara Ayash, still lean and attractive with a girlish smile, recalled the fantasy world she had plunged into when she finally said "yes." "At first we set up housekeeping in Hollywood, in a luxurious apartment that had once been Mike Todd's. It was huge. There was plenty of room for my kids, two girls and two boys from six to thirteen. I loved the big living room with its white piano.

"I remember the first time he took me shopping. He decided he wanted to buy me some clothes. Whenever I used to go shopping, I was always hunting for bargains. The most I'd ever paid was fourteen or sixteen dollars for a dress. He took me to an exclusive salon where there were no price tags on the clothes and he insisted that I pick out four outfits. When the saleswoman handed him the bill, it was for $4,000! I couldn't believe it. I couldn't sleep that night thinking about spending all that money on clothes. I ended up sobbing over the waste, thinking how the money could have been spent.

"At first it was hard for me to conceive of spending money that way. I just couldn't accept it. But I later found it was an easy trap to fall into. When we moved to a mansion in the Los Angeles suburbs, I spent another $30,000 decorating it. After a few years I got to feel that there was a never-ending supply of money, and I was learning to spend.

"I got a Cadillac and a station wagon, and he had a Continental, and as soon as they were old enough, all the kids got cars of their own. I bought a 1904 antique Steinway piano for $13,000. We had a billiard room, a library, a swimming pool, and stables. On a whim we'd catch a jet to Europe and stay for three or four weeks or fly to New York to see a play, or to Las Vegas.

"We were constantly throwing parties for 60 people or more, serving filet mignon at four in the morning to sober them up. I remember in the morning we used to find diamond rings on the bottom of the pool.

"The spending was ridiculous. I'd be out shopping and something like an electric massager would catch my eye and I'd buy six—one for everybody in the family. We spent money on jewelry, horses, exotic pets, a houseboat, a fishing boat, a huge camper and a dune buggy, and lots of vacations. At Christmas we would spend thousands for lights just to keep up with the neighbors, and our tree would be eighteen feet high.

"It got to the point that when birthdays came we really didn't know what to give one another, because we already had so much. I remember one year I solved the problem by having gold neck chains made for the prize bandy chickens that my husband raised as a hobby. He once gave me a $15,000 recording session for my birthday. I was toying with music and had written four songs. He hired a singer and musicians and studio and had them recorded. Piles of the albums sat in the garage for a long time.

"I didn't like some of the things that were happening. I was becoming very demanding. I'd forget to make an appointment at the beauty salon and then I'd just telephone at the last minute and say, 'It's worth an extra $50 if you'll take me right away.' And of course they'd put me ahead of someone else.

"The kids were getting spoiled. They weren't taking care of their things. I had given one of my daughters a bracelet made of valuable old Spanish coins—worth over $3,000—and she just misplaced it. Their clothes, with all the best labels, would end up in heaps on the floor, and before, when they were just wearing hand-me-downs, believe me, they used to take care of their clothes. They would burn out the engine on a car and it wouldn't worry them; they'd just order a new engine.

"A lot of things began to bother me. My husband would be off in Texas or somewhere for four or five days, and I didn't dare ask what he was doing, did he have a girlfriend. If I asked, he'd say, 'I'm busy making money for you.'

"There were things I wanted to tell him, but we weren't really communicating. There were always people around. People were always approaching him with schemes and I wanted to say, 'These people come to you, bend to you and respect you, but all they want is some of your money.'

"Despite all the money we had, I still felt insecure. I couldn't understand why I wasn't enjoying my life the way I thought I should be. I couldn't find things to occupy my time.

"I'd call up friends and we'd go to lunch or shopping, or I'd go to the beauty shop, or do volunteer work. Once I wanted to sew a dress for myself, and when I told my husband he laughed and said, 'Why should you sew when you can buy any dress you want?'

"I did a lot of bowling then, several days a week. It was something I liked to do. But I learned I couldn't mix my bowling buddies with our rich friends. Inviting them to the same parties didn't work. The bowling alley people would drink and one of them would throw one of our rich friends, mink and all, into the pool. And they didn't converse on the same level. Our rich friends would make the bowling people feel inferior, and the rich people would complain that it was unforgivable to mix the two sets of people. Some of them, when I'd invite them to another party, would want to know who else was going to be there.

"One day in 1972 this whole life came crashing to an end. Bob sat me down and poured me a cup of coffee and handed me the morning paper, the *Los Angeles Times*. I couldn't believe it. There was a story reporting that he'd been charged with income tax evasion.

"It never occurred to me that we had any money problems. He sheltered me from it completely. He explained to me that business had fallen off in recent years and he hadn't wanted to worry me about it; he admitted he'd been cutting corners on taxes and he told me he had been afraid that if the money wasn't there he might lose me.

"The government claimed he owed $400,000 in taxes, which would mean the house would have to go, the cars, the furniture, everything, but even then I couldn't believe that he might actually have to go to jail. I refused to believe it even when they sentenced him. I thought men who had money could get out of anything. We tried lawyers all over the country and when the last of the money was gone, and the jewelry pawned, I drove him in an old used car to the Terminal Island Federal Prison and he began his sentence.

"At that moment all I had was the car, a month's rent paid in advance on a small apartment, and seven dollars. I had worked as a waitress and in dime stores since I was fourteen, though, so I thought I could get a job right away. But I tried everywhere and couldn't get anything, not even as a desk girl in a bowling alley.

"I was completely broke, and I had to do something. I ended up in the welfare office, which to me was the worst thing left to happen. As I stood in line with a handful of papers they had given me, I got sick to my stomach. I ran out of there, went home, crawled into my bed and cried until I slept.

"When I awoke I had a strange compulsion to fix my nails. I'd always had a sense of perfection about manicuring and thought I did my own nails better than the professionals. Some of my friends agreed, and once in a while I had done a manicure for a good friend because I was proud that I did it so well. The phone rang and a friend was asking me to go bowling with her; they were short one girl on the team, but I made excuses and suggested someone else. She told me the other woman had a date with a manicurist to have her nails done for $45.

"That gave me the idea that started me in business. I began doing nails for friends and after a while one of them decided to back me in opening a little shop. Through the shop, through my work, my faith in myself—which all the money we had couldn't buy—gradually built up. I was supporting myself and the family.

"Today my goals are to pay the rent, eat, enjoy the work I'm doing, and express what I am through my work. I really enjoy it, the relations, the conversations, and the esteem I feel. It wasn't something given to me. It's something I built.

"My husband is free now. He started with a job in a furniture store and he's already managing it. He's a brilliant man. He's made and lost a fortune and he intends to make it again. I don't know how I feel about that. I don't feel it's necessary, but he does. I do know that if he does make it again I won't say no to it, but I won't attach the same importance to it. We've got each other, and we've got a lifetime.

"Because I stuck by him, he's learned that he meant more to me than wealth, and I personally found that money hadn't made me feel secure. Only *I* could do that."

Sex and money traditionally have been as intertwined in life as in the marriage contract itself, one version of which states, "And I thee with all my worldly goods endow"—a pledge as often honored in the divorce courts as in the home.

Psychiatrists remind us that in the family, the male generally decides money matters *and* initiates sexual activity, assuming the upper hand through the power of his economic dominance over his wife. Similarly, in courtship, it is the man who pays, and even in marriage it is not unusual for men to reward their wives with material goods for sexual favors—with varying degrees of subtlety.

Society tends to equate money and potency. Possessions such as powerful automobiles, luxurious living accommodations, and fine clothing—as well as the respect of the subservient which money can buy—are demonstrations of virility. Female beauty, when regarded as a commodity, historically carries a bartering value.

The idea of marrying millions—encouraged by generations of mothers who hope to spare their daughters the dire
financial lessons they themselves have learned—usually
avoids the accusation of being cold-blooded calculation with
the rationale that "It's just as easy to fall in love with a rich
man." As a vocation, the idea of marrying for money has
become tarnished in this enlightened age, but Mother, we
hasten to add, wasn't entirely wrong. The wealthy man—
though sometimes older and physically less well-endowed
than the Golden Boys that many females dream of—generally
has the marks of accomplishment, the worldly wisdom, and
the access to pleasurable things, that can make him lovable
enough to "sweep a girl off her feet."

Nevertheless, our culture warns us through novels, films,
television melodramas, and countless heartthrob magazines
that the woman who marries just for money—neglecting
the urgings of her heart—stands in grave peril of getting
money and nothing more.

Irene Glendon was one of five girls in a group of
beauties who graduated from school together and who began
their dating days by comparing notes and hopes. She declared
from the start that the man she married would be wealthy,
and that nothing would budge her from this resolve.

One by one, all the other girls married men of their
choice. At the age of 27 and in obvious danger of not succeed-
ing in her avowed plan of action, Irene still pursued her
dream with a cold determination that sometimes put off her
friends. She worked for a living but spent every cent to
purchase the best of clothes from the best shops. She avoided
middle-class parties and social events, going only to the best
hotels and restaurants, the best country clubs, and upper-class
activities, where there were most likely to be men who qual-
ified for the position she had in mind.

By then, her girlfriends were shaking their heads and
saying how sad it was about Irene and her pretensions; obviously, it would never work. Any romance fan could tell her
that. Either she was doomed to frigid old maidenhood or,

abandoning her course in her failing years (she wasn't getting any younger), she would cave in and marry someone who was not only poor, but stingy to boot.

Nevertheless, at 28, and to everyone's surprise, Irene announced her forthcoming marriage to a kindly, soft-spoken millionaire. He was a "self-made" man who had been too preoccupied with getting rich to socialize much, but Irene led him out of his shell, teaching him to spend money with the same devotion he'd shown for acquiring it.

They live in a mansion overlooking Los Angeles and there they have raised four children with all the warmth of loving parents, roles Irene and her husband espoused with total commitment. Her husband is devoted to her and gives her everything her heart desires. Their love for each other after years of marriage is strong and supportive.

Meanwhile, most of Irene's friends had been divorced and were seeking—with varying determination and altered standards—men who would fulfill their needs.

You figure it out!

When she married Jack Reins, Marisa Reins set out to shop for a house, but she really didn't know what they could afford. "What should I look for?" she asked her husband. "What section of town? It can make a big difference in price."

"Why don't you just look until you find something you like, and then we'll see," he answered.

She knew he liked to entertain a lot for business, and she knew the importance of a "good address," so she started at the top, in Beverly Hills, if only to treat herself to a glimpse of the sumptuous palaces tucked away behind iron gates on the most expensive real estate in Southern California. She made the rounds, ushered by real estate agents whose coolness suggested their certainty that she could not afford the magnificent estates she asked to be shown. She was afraid they were right.

"One of the houses I saw today," she told her husband

that night, "was just incredible. A long, winding driveway, more like a highway lined with poplar trees, and you go over a hill just before you reach this gigantic white house that looks like Monticello or maybe the Beverly Hills Library—pillars and statues and fountains and pools everywhere. The living room is as big as a dance hall."

She added, in jest, "But I told the agent, 'Only eighteen rooms? It wouldn't do!' "

Her husband looked up and said, "How much was it?"

"They were *only* asking a million."

To her amazement, he promptly wrote a check for that amount.

It was a giant step up in lifestyle for the young woman who had come to California as a teenager married to a serviceman, both migrants from the Midwest, from one of America's poorest counties. At the age of 22 she'd found herself divorced, trying to support two children on a $60-a-week receptionist's job.

She had been a shapely, eye-catching redhead with ambition and—like thousands of beautiful young women who flock to the Los Angeles area—she was not untouched by the dream of becoming a star. Why not? She had the looks, she knew that. It was only a matter of getting started. She had determined to ask her friends, "How *do* you get started?"

One friend had sent pictures of her—eight-by-ten glossies that really looked professional—to a local amusement park, smaller but similar to Disneyland. When she received a telephone call asking her to come for a job interview, she knew in her heart that it was the start of a fabulous career. What they needed was a pretty young woman to do no more than strike alluring poses and wave, scantily clad, in front of their main attraction. But the job paid five times what she had been earning as a receptionist, and the number of competitors for the opening had almost added up to the amount of dollars involved. She took it joyfully.

And, in storybook fashion, her next step to stardom had emerged from that stepping-stone. An agent had seen her,

had talked a movie studio into offering her a contract, and
she signed it almost without noticing that it meant a cut in pay.
Only temporarily, of course.

The exciting world of Hollywood beckoned, and she
had been paraded through the publicity mill of beauty con-
tests, special appearances for studio promotions, and just "being seen" at the popular restaurants and film premieres. She
had advanced to playing minor roles in films destined for the
second half of double features, always, it seemed, in the role
of someone's anonymous girlfriend or equally anonymous
murder victim.

Somehow, the next step, the big one, had never quite
materialized for Marisa. She had enjoyed the comforts of a
nice home and regular pay through her contract, but her
uncertainty about her future had grown. Then one night, at
one of the "in" nightclubs of the "Beautiful People," she met
Jack Reins, and suddenly her "career" seemed somehow less
important to her than it had before.

After fourteen years of marriage, Mrs. Reins still pre-
sides happily over her home, which is as impressive and or-
derly as a museum. Winding staircase, large crystal chan-
delier, grand piano, and graceful furniture in muted colors.
A wall of glass exposes the green yard bejeweled with an
Olympic-size swimming pool that glistens in the afternoon
sun.

Fortyish, her figure a shade fuller than it was in the
stunning stills of her filmland days, she enters the living
room, casual in jeans and a T-shirt topped by a colorful over-
blouse. She displays a cover-girl smile and her pink complexion recalls those of the stars of early technicolor musicals. Her
maid serves white wine in delicate stemware and she speaks
in an ebullient manner:

"I liked Jack from the moment I met him, because he's
such an exciting, brilliant man—a self-made man. From the
start we spoke as if we'd known each other for years.

"One of the best things about being married to him is all
the interesting people around. In one trip to Europe we met a

queen, a prince, and a princess. We meet celebrities, writers, industrialists, politicians. People whose names are in the papers every day stop by when they're in town or come to our parties.

"Jack says I'm a great asset to him. I'm outgoing. I meet people well. He likes to talk to me; we even talk about his business. It must show that we're really happy. Wealth is just the icing on the cake.

"When I first married Jack, he opened a joint checking account for us and told me to write checks whenever I pleased. It was a great feeling to realize there never would be a worry about money. But, even though I don't have to think about whether or not something's expensive before I buy it, I still do. Despite our money, I'm still very frugal. Jack can't believe it.

"For instance, I hate shopping for clothes, which seems to be the main pastime for some of the women I know. I do buy some designer clothes, but I consider it a rip-off because you're just paying for the prestige of the label. Still, I do indulge myself in some special things—a beautiful sculpture, a telephone for my Mercedes, a stained glass window.

"Before we were married, my friends mostly were kooky show business people. His friends are society people, but they are always nice to me. His friends, the men, talk mostly business at parties and the women talk about domestic problems, but there are so many different, interesting people in different fields that it's never boring.

"I work with many charities. If it weren't for wealthy people, how could charities keep going? Most wealthy people I know give much more to charities than they can deduct in taxes, and they give their time, too.

"I'm an advocate of the American Dream. I always felt that one day I'd be wealthy, a big success, but I thought I'd do it by myself.

"I still keep in touch with my roots, the people back home, by visiting my family and friends there. It's such a poverty-stricken area. But one of my sisters there says she wouldn't swap for my lifestyle, always being around so many people.

"Maybe that's the biggest disadvantage of our lives now. We have so many friends, we're just too busy socially. I never seem to have the time to organize and accomplish what I want. I've been like caught up in a whirlwind. I want to stop and contribute something meaningful. I want to have a sense of accomplishment.

"I know a lot of wives of wealthy men who seem perfectly happy just being wives and nothing more." Fixing her eyes vaguely in the splendor of her surroundings, where somewhere in the background a cook, houseman, and maid attended their respective tasks, she added, "I would not be satisfied being just a housewife."

Generally speaking, the higher the income, the greater the chance for stability in marriage, according to a 1977 survey conducted nationally by Dr. Stephen J. Bahr, associate professor, Department of Sociology, Brigham Young University. He interviewed 1,257 women each year for five years, and based his findings on the number of marriages still intact at the end of the five years.

Dr. Bahr measured income and assets in the marriages involved and regarded occupation and education as factors contributing to the income, stating, "Whether socioeconomic status is measured by occupation, income, education, or a combination of these does not alter the basic finding of a decrease in the divorce rate as socioeconomic status increases."

Certainly the possession of "means" lightens many of the potential areas of conflict between married people, especially when we consider the prominence of money matters among the problems that lead to divorce.

"When people are poor, their energies are devoted to sustaining themselves," observed Dr. Arnold Gilberg, a Beverly Hills psychiatrist. "When the affluent state arrives, then love, affection, caring—the quality of life—gets priority.

"Sexual dissatisfaction is something you hear from the middle class. The lower class has more pressing arguments than the quality of orgasm, and the upper class can deal with it—they can buy a solution."

Obviously, the well-to-do can benefit from psychiatric treatment that might be out of the question for those on a restricted budget. But the availability of large sums of money for psychiatry is no guarantee that the course of even true love among the rich ever will run smooth.

Tricia, aged 32, works as a receptionist. It's been four years since the attractive, blue-eyed brunette was divorced, but she finds herself much happier now than she was in her earlier wealthy life:

"I was a secretary for an insurance office when I met my husband, and I was still living with my family. He was a handsome executive, and he acted as if he had money to spend. I was delighted to hear he was a multimillionaire, but luxury was not that important to me. Most of all I wanted love, and I thought I found it with him.

"When we became engaged, he bought me a new Lincoln Continental, and I'd been driving an old Ford up to then. We moved to a penthouse apartment and six months later, when we got married, we bought the big house they used as William Holden's place in the film *Breezy*,—four bedrooms, three acres. Last year I noticed it was up for sale again for about $600,000.

"While we were married I traveled all over the country with my husband—Hawaii, Puerto Rico, and always first class. I never thought about the luxuries I had while I had them.

"But he was always traveling. We were apart so much. And when he did come home, I'd have this sick anticipation about when he'd be leaving again. I would have traded all the luxuries if he just could have been a plumber or something and could have been home every night.

"In the last two years of our marriage I wanted a smaller, more homey type of home, so he got it for me. The big house had been more of a showplace; a decorator had done it. I was happier in the smaller home, which was an old barn that we decorated ourselves. Since the divorce I've developed my own lifestyle, which includes working and doing things for myself. We're still good friends and at times I miss *him*, but not what he *had*."

We prefer our fantasies neat, but life is not. Even a romantic dream-come-true more likely will fall somewhere between the Cinderella story and the unfulfilled heroine Maude Muller's longing for "what might have been."

But a million-dollar husband can easily fit into a perfect marriage. It seems to depend on the people, not the money.

For instance, there was a good-hearted cocktail waitress in Las Vegas who caught her boss's eye one day. She was 32 and he was 65, but she happened to be attracted to older men. He not only owned the cocktail lounge, but the hotel it was in and a couple of others besides.

From the ranks of service, waiting on tables, she was swept off her feet and plunged into a society whirl, but instead of feeling out of place, she accepted things naturally, and she, in turn, was accepted for her naturalness, her lack of pretension. In the four years since their marriage she has traveled all over America, to Europe a few times, the Orient and elsewhere, and she turns the trips into buying excursions, picking up unusual articles with which to stock a gift shop she plans to open as a hobby.

Wealthy women often complain that they have nothing to do, that they feel unfulfilled. Said one woman after returning from an exclusive resort where the rich go to lose weight, "All I heard from all these affluent women at that fat farm was the same gripe: 'I'm frustrated. Something's missing in my life.' We had everything society said we should have to be happy—beautiful homes, families, household help, everything the All-American woman should have—and still there was a great void in our lives."

But the lack of fulfillment experienced by so many

women knows no class barriers. Except for the added aware-
ness and potential that wealth brings, the problem affects
underemployed poorer women as well as the wealthy.

Beth Ann Clutter sat at her key-punch machine with a far-
away look in her dark eyes. For a moment she was oblivious to
the office noises around her. She wasn't thinking about the
senior prom, though it was coming up soon, or what college
she'd go to after graduating from David Douglas High in
Portland, Oregon. Her mind had drifted to the kind of ad-
ventures she might have when she took off traveling after
graduation with the money she'd saved from her after-school
job as a key-punch operator.

A striking seventeen-year-old whose delicate features
were set off by a cap of curly hair, she had a spirited, independent nature that set her apart from schoolmates with conventional plans for a job, marriage, or college after graduation. She was longing to spice her life with a taste of exotic
lands and people, far from the modest, middle-class home
where she lived with her mother, stepfather, two brothers,
and sister.

Shortly after graduation the teenager flew to Honolulu
for a visit with her father, Robert Clutter. During the summer, they were invited to spend a few weeks on the island of
Kauai, Hawaii, with Howard Taylor, the brother of actress
Elizabeth Taylor, who worked with Clutter in the oceanog-
raphy department of the University of Hawaii in Honolulu.

At the Taylor home, Beth met a handsome, dark-haired
youth about a year younger than she, Michael Wilding, Jr.,
son of Elizabeth Taylor. Their affection for each other grew,
and they found they shared a common dream: they decided
to pool their money and travel together. They flew to Europe
and made their way to the Middle East and India, traveling on
trains, living in cheap hotels, and somehow managing on
about five dollars a day. It was a hippie existence they shared

with other young people. They managed to finance their travels partly with the money she'd saved, and Michael would call his mother from time to time to ask for money.

In India, after nearly a year of traveling, they decided they'd had enough. They made a phone call to Elizabeth, and flew to join her in the south of France.

Beth was looking forward to meeting Michael's mother, but she was very nervous on the plane trip. She wondered if the famous actress would like her. She forgot her fears as Miss Taylor welcomed her warmly with a lovely bouquet of flowers. They went to a beautiful little restaurant in Nice and had pizza and beer and talked and talked. It had been a long time since Miss Taylor had seen her wandering son and it was obvious that she was overjoyed at their reunion. To Beth's delight, she and Miss Taylor hit it off from the start.

It was as though the famed actress was their special genie who with a wave of her checkbook had the power to transform their world from small, dreary hotel rooms and meager meals to living in the most luxurious hotels and dining on gourmet food with a retinue of staff to see to their every need.

The Oregon teenager joined Elizabeth on her yacht, where she met her son Christopher and daughter Liza for the first time. Maria (Elizabeth and Burton's adopted daughter) was away at school and Burton (to whom the star was married at the time) was in London.

On October 6, 1970, just two weeks after her first meeting with the Taylor clan, Beth and Michael were married in Caxton Hall in London. They had undergone a grand transformation for the wedding. The teenagers who had knocked around for months in scruffy jeans and shirts were now resplendent, with Beth in a long, white chiffon gown and flowers in her hair and Michael wearing a maroon velvet caftan with matching bellbottoms.

After the ceremony Miss Taylor gave a champagne reception for the newlyweds in the posh Dorchester Hotel. A crush of photographers and fans vied to get closer to the wedding party. For Beth it was like a formal initiation into the Taylor-Burton "magic" circle. The next day photos and headlines around the world proclaimed the wedding of the young woman who just months before was an anonymous Portland high school co-ed.

The young couple honeymooned in a luxurious suite at the Dorchester, just down the hall from the Burtons. It was a far cry from the hotels they'd called home during their travels, where "down the hall" usually meant the location of the community bathroom.

Richard's wedding present to the couple was a $70,000 townhouse, and together Elizabeth and Richard gave Michael and Beth a Jaguar sports car. Elizabeth also gave them money to get started on.

The actress seemed to enjoy showering Beth with gifts, surprising her with breathtaking designer outfits, or inviting a designer to send over part of a collection of clothes from which Beth could choose what she liked. Elizabeth especially liked giving Beth frilly, chiffon-type gowns and expensive jewelry. Several times a year the young Wildings would stay with the Burtons or travel with them in their grand manner, and Beth was dazzled by their lifestyle.

Though she had warm feelings for Miss Taylor from the start, she sometimes wondered if the actress might have wanted someone better for her son because she was not from the wealthy class. Feelings of inferiority worried Beth, but her mother-in-law's kindness soon enabled her to feel more a part of the family.

Beth liked Burton as well and found he was very good with Elizabeth's and his children. He would prod their minds. He wanted to talk to them and understand them. At Christmastime he would tell them Welsh Christmas stories. Knowing how much Beth liked to read, he introduced her to a series of books on anthropology that he thought were especially good. Beth had expected that Christopher, Liza, and

Maria might be snobbish; but she found them casual and friendly and, though they didn't spend much time with their mother, they had a warm relationship with her.

To Beth all her new experiences with wealth and glamour were like a silver thread suddenly interwoven in her life. But her marriage quickly began to tarnish. While she had considered their hippie romp through Europe and the Middle East a wonderful—but completed—adventure it appeared that Michael sincerely wished to continue following that lifestyle. Beth knew she wanted to settle into a secure family relationship, and this honest difference of values put a great strain on their marriage.

Since her own mother was so far away, Beth was grateful that she could turn to Elizabeth for understanding, and she soon had need of it. When Beth discovered she was pregnant, she became very upset. She telephoned her mother-in-law, who was yachting in the Mediterranean, to tell her how weak and confused she felt under the circumstances. But Miss Taylor, overjoyed at the prospect of having her first grandchild, assured Beth that everything would turn out well and that she always would be there whenever Beth needed her.

Beth gave birth to her daughter Leyla in a small, private maternity clinic in London. Although Elizabeth and Burton were in another country at the time, they flew to London as soon as they got the news. Miss Taylor gave the baby a beautiful bassinette, a crib, and toys, and even some Christian Dior clothes. She played with the infant constantly and even enjoyed bathing the child.

But the end of these idyllic family scenes was drawing near.

One day, after an apparently ordinary husband-and-wife spat, Beth packed her things, took Leyla and left, going first to Elizabeth's house and then to Hawaii. She finally moved back in Portland, where she started divorce proceedings which Michael did not contest.

Having experienced the effervescence of a jet-set life with Michael, Beth has since remarried, and now like her new husband, she works as a hairdresser, and lives in a small house in Portland.

They're just memories now, the jaunts to the playgrounds of the "Beautiful People" in Switzerland, Rome, London, Mexico, the luxury suites in famous hotels, the costly gifts from Elizabeth, the servants, the fawning attention of waiters, desk clerks, chauffeurs . . .

Relaxing finally after her nine-to-five day at the Magnum Opus Beauty Salon, picking up her daughter Leyla at the home of her mother, who cares for her during the day, and getting dinner on the table for her small family, she thought about her experiences as a kind of modern-day Cinderella. "Sometimes," she said, "I look back on the luxury I once had and think how I'd like it again." She held out her hand to show off a lovely antique diamond ring. "This is one of the gifts Elizabeth gave me, and I treasure it. But I think I'm happier spiritually now. My husband and I are working together toward our goal of opening our own beauty shop. It can be hard work, and frustrating. But this sharing of a goal and communication is an important ingredient in this marriage. All the things that money can buy can't make up for that."

5. The Bright Idea

The small, cramped Chinese market was crowded with an exotic array of canned foods, fruits, and vegetables, some of which Anita Benson had never seen before. Slowly she walked up and down the aisles intrigued by the strange labels, lulled by the sing-song chatter of the Oriental women shoppers and, for the moment, gratefully far removed from the wide sterile aisles of her neighborhood supermarket and its droning piped-in music.

That sunny afternoon, she'd decided to spend a few hours just wandering around the Chinese section. As usual, her inclinations took her off the beaten path, away from the touristy Chinatown where for blocks on end souvenir shops alternated monotonously with restaurants. Instead she strolled down the narrow streets of the real Chinese district, losing herself in the sights and sounds of another culture and escaping for a while the reality of her own world.

A pretty, artistic, and headstrong divorcee in her mid-

119

twenties, she'd recently returned home after two years of "bumming around," and she had no idea what direction her life should now take. She felt she had tremendous ability and drive—the "success karma," as she called it. But what to focus on? She was a little disenchanted. She knew she wasn't getting anywhere; she was just treading water. Her money was running out and she knew she'd have to find some kind of work to support herself pretty quickly.

At the far end of the market she noticed empty rice sacks piled up fifteen feet high against a wall. Fascinated by the beauty of their Oriental lettering and their colorful floral design, she impulsively said to herself, "I must make something out of these."

It was a ludicrous idea, considering she hardly ever sewed. (In fact, she'd flunked sewing in school.) But the sacks were so attractive that she believed she could surely do something special with them. A clerk told her the 25- and 50-pound rice sacks were empties that piled up one by one as rice was transferred into smaller containers for sale. She asked if she could buy some of the empties. He laughed and charged her twenty-five cents each for a few of them.

When she got the sacks home she unstitched them and cut up the material to try to put together a little jean-style jacket similar to the ones she always wore with her blue jeans. She traced the line of her jacket on the rice sack material and stitched it painstakingly by hand. It turned out surprisingly well. When she showed it to friends, their reaction was unanimous: "Wow! That's fantastic!"

And it *was* a knockout. When she sauntered into a smart clothing store a few days later, the owner, mistaking her for a fashion designer, praised the jacket as a work of art. He wanted to sell jackets like that. How many of them could she deliver? How soon? She walked out of the store with an order for a hundred of them, without the faintest idea of how to fill the order, and only a little more than a hundred dollars left to her name for capital.

The chic little shop was willing to pay her $22 each for a hundred of the jackets, and the owner had suggested, "You really ought to make pants to go with them. I'd buy those, too."

That was in the early 1970's, and almost overnight Mrs. Benson became head of her own garment business, which expanded by leaps and bounds into a multimillion-dollar success. She recalled the start:

"After I got that first order I went all over town getting more. By the end of the first week I had orders for $15,000 worth of the jackets. My big problem now was finding a way to produce them.

"On the rice sacks I found the name of the company that sold them and I convinced the owner to sell me the sacks for fifteen cents each. Friends helped me cut the stitching that formed the material into sacks. And I found a lady who would sew each jacket pattern for $3.25. I'd deliver the finished jackets to the store, they'd pay me, I'd pay my sewing lady, buy more sacks and continue like that. I had the little business really cooking, working out of my one-bedroom apartment, with rice sacks and thread everywhere.

"I worked long hours and friends kidded me about never taking time to enjoy myself anymore. But, I knew I'd finally found a way to make it big. As the money for the jackets started coming in, I rented a workshop for $62 a month. I got a couple of ladies to work there and crank out these jackets for me. I even started making pants to match.

"I learned the business as I went along and by the end of the first year I'd sold $100,000 in clothes. The second year we did $1.5 million, and last January was our sixth year and we earned about $6 million. We now have over a hundred employees.

"Lots of money sets you free in a special way. You're able to fulfill a lot of fantasy in your life. For example, I always wanted to go down the Amazon River, so I chartered a boat and did it, damn it! Another of my childhood fantasies was to

visit with the South American Indians and I hopped on a
plane and achieved that. I visited places like Europe, North
Africa, and the Orient too.

"I've bought myself fabulous clothes. And, as soon as I
was into the money I bought myself a Mercedes. I went crazy
buying jewels like two-carat diamond earrings for $5,000.

"I splurged on a fabulous, 25-year-old house and had it
made over into a very exotic villa that looks like a Moroccan
palace with tile floors and arches and a magnificent view.

"One of the greatest joys the money gave me was en-
abling me to track down my natural mother and father. I'd
been adopted when I was six months old, and for many years
I dreamed of finding the couple who brought me into the
world. With all this money I could afford to travel around the
country and search for them and even hire a detective to help
me. I found out I had been born in a small town in Texas, so I
placed ads about my search in newspapers in every city in
Texas. Through one of those ads I found a judge who
opened my sealed records. As a result I tracked down my
mother in Washington and my father in Texas.

"I flew to meet each of them and they were so happy I
found them. My mother explained she gave me up because
she was not married to my father and was too poor to give me
a good home. She said for years she dreamed of finding me
but had given up hope that it would be possible."

Though her sudden wealth has brought her a great deal
of joy, Anita is frank about the drawbacks of having suddenly
achieved money and power on her own.

"There's a certain loneliness that comes with getting
wealthy in this way," she pointed out. "You've got all this
responsibility. The major decisions of the business rest on
your shoulders. There's no one else to turn to for answers.

"Also, because of my business I'm often in the position
of having to socialize with people I ordinarily wouldn't want
to get that friendly with. They're people involved in my business dealings.

"And, I've found men's attitudes have changed toward me. Many men are intimidated by a woman with my strong and driving image. But the kind of men who would be intimidated by me wouldn't interest me anyway. I meet a lot of interesting men in my business dealings and usually date lawyers, bankers, and businessmen. I have a boyfriend who's also made a success of a business he started. I'm not sold on the idea of him exclusively, though."

Like many newly rich people, Anita found friends and employees looking to her for loans. "This started soon after I began making a lot of money," she said. "I've always had a very generous nature. But it just got to be too much, and I don't make loans any more.

"Working to keep all this money coming in puts a lot of pressure on me and makes my life very hectic. Where before I always was ready to go out and party, now I really appreciate the time I spend alone at home unwinding in front of the television or just staring into space."

Though one of her favorite forms of recreation is going on sprees with her boyfriend in which they try to outbuy each other, she confides, "The best thing about my business is not all the things I can buy with the money I earn, but the fact that it's enabled me to find a direction for my drive and talent."

More new millionaires emerge from the ranks of business than any other, and, of those who make it suddenly, most do it through a brilliant idea that's timely enough to catch on in the world of commerce. The Hula Hoop, the Pet Rock, McDonald's, the Polaroid Land camera, the Frisbee and Pong come to mind as outstanding examples. Some of these are of fad proportions, but others seem to have made a mark as lasting fixtures on the American scene.

Novelties, franchises, and real estate stand out as the most wide-open fields for quick riches, although occasionally

artistic creations such as books, record albums, and films have
scored quickly without a major investment on the part of their
originators.

Most of the fortunes that are made in business accumu-
late gradually, however, over long periods of time, with trial
and error showing the way, and for every story of overnight
success there are dozens of stories about ventures that failed
somewhere in the chain from concept, to financing, to production, to distribution, to marketing.

When a Midwestern mixing machine salesman named
Ray Kroc became curious about why one drive-in located in
San Bernardino, California, ordered six of the items he sold
while most hamburger joints made do with one, he went back
for a closer look and discovered that the tiny hamburger joint
was also selling ten times as many burgers, hot dogs, milk
shakes, and soft drinks as any other outlet its size. He was
especially intrigued with their mass-production techniques
that served a customer almost as quickly as his order could be
taken. From that little drive-in began the burgeoning,
billion-dollar business that placed "golden arches" and the
name McDonald's in every community in America as well as
many around the world.

When a former encyclopedia salesman in Louisville
named John Y. Brown talked the aging Colonel Sanders into
divulging and selling out his unique fried chicken recipe,
most every populated thoroughfare in the country soon
began sprouting a giant bucket twirling over outlets selling
Kentucky Fried Chicken to take-out customers, eventually
permitting the tall, handsome Brown, the real franchise king,
to sell his interests in the operation for $35 million—about
one million for every year of his age. Let the Colonel play
figurehead; it was Brown's franchise idea that really sold
America on chicken and made him rich.

Dr. Edwin Land, a Cambridge, Massachusetts, scientist,
was still in his forties when he perfected the Polaroid camera
and convinced businessmen of its market potential. It wasn't
an easy task, technically or in the selling. Said one early poten-

tial stockholder, "They offered me all kinds of stock options, but I said to myself, 'Who's going to buy a little toy camera that develops its own pictures?' " That was singer Perry Como, former barber, who nevertheless agreed to do commercials for the "toy" because some friends asked him to, as a favor. He moaned years later, "I put my money in the Edsel, instead."

The businessmen behind great film ideas know the awful risks of ventures that hinge on public emotion, but they are enticed by the fantastic bonanzas awarded the successful. Ingo Preminger, a New York agent who had never made a film before, telephoned the young Richard Zanuck one day shortly after the latter's father, Darryl, had put him in charge of the flagging Twentieth Century-Fox studios. Preminger, excitement in his voice, urged Zanuck to read a book, a comedy set in the Korean War. Zanuck, sifting through endless piles of script submissions at poolside in California, responded politely but rolled his eyes in hopelessness as he hung up. When Preminger persisted in messengering the book, Zanuck flipped through it, read it, and decided to make the film *M.A.S.H.* Later, after the film earned more than ten times its investment of $3 million within a year, Zanuck mused: "Some people can walk into a bookstore unemployed and walk out as a producer. . . . In his very first outing as a producer, Ingo became an incredibly rich man. You can be a producer all your life and never hit it that big."

Television actor Michael Douglas, who took over the task of trying to get financial backing and a good script to film *One Flew Over the Cuckoo's Nest* after his father, Kirk, an industry giant, had failed, clicked with a rock music millionaire and in his first venture as a co-producer saw the film rack up an unbelievable $100 million in its first year. As if stunned, the young Douglas pondered, "In one film I made more money than my father earned in a lifetime as a star."

Gary Dahl, who lived in a tiny cabin in the Santa Cruz, California, mountains with his wife, came up with an idea, an invention. Actually it was a joke, but he was proud of it. It satirized the $2 billion pet industry in America and somehow he believed the country had enough of a sense of humor to go along with the joke. Several years ago, between Labor Day and Christmas, he became a millionaire selling something anybody could pick up in their own back yard: rocks. The Pet Rock fad—a box with a stone and a humorous training booklet—captured the fancy of a million buyers in America at a retail price of nearly four dollars. He admitted, "Naturally the production costs were small."

Another San Francisco area young man, Nolan Bushnell, visualized his wealth in the form of a game and started a company called Atari in 1972 with an investment of $500, plus considerable technical expertise. The next year his company sold $11 million worth of the television game Pong, and a few years later he liquidated his interests in the operation for $28 million.

In Colorado there's a young couple who many people would have called hippies because of their clothes and lifestyle, but they liked to consider themselves backwoods people, returning to the earth. And in the earth, they struck it rich. When they heard that oil and coal leases on government land nearby were to be awarded on the basis of a drawing, at pennies per acre, they were smart enough to realize that nothing in the law said that they, as private individuals, couldn't compete with the giant oil companies. They placed their bid, and when it was drawn, they turned around and sold it a few days later for hundreds of thousands of dollars.

But most business income, by the very cautious nature of investors who usually are needed to launch a venture, comes slowly and steadily, not overnight.

The tall, slim, soft-spoken multimillionaire Kirk Kirkorian rose from the sweltering farmland area of Bakersfield, California, and fought 38 amateur bouts before and during World War II. After the war he started trading surplus aircraft parts, then whole airplanes, and then airlines, building up a fortune that put him in the position to buy and sell Las Vegas hotels, a career culminated a few years ago with the purchase of Metro-Goldwyn-Mayer film studios and construction of the largest hotel in the gambling capital, the MGM Grand.

He commented on the transition from poor to rich, "I don't know—there never was a time I would have thought of making a million dollars. At one time, maybe, I'd have been content with $200 a month. When I reached $50,000 a year, that was a big thing in my life, but even then I didn't think beyond that. I just grew into it."

When Paul Fegen was a teenager, he knew exactly what he wanted in life: girls. Beautiful girls. Young girls. Girls with curvaceous bodies and lovely faces. Girls with charm and personality. Tall girls, short girls. Blondes, brunettes. Girls with long hair and girls with short hair. But above all, girls who would like him. Love him. And, preferably, who would fall all over him.

But that, as he knew, was a dream unlikely to be fulfilled. In 1950, when he was sixteen years old and a student at Los Angeles High School, girls didn't behave that way, especially toward a guy who was—like him—so exceedingly average. His nose was a little long, and maybe his chin was a little long, or maybe it was just that his whole head was a little long, he sometimes thought during his regular self-critical mirror inspections. Being a realist, he knew women wouldn't throw themselves at Paul Fegen for his looks.

And it wouldn't be for his money, either, because he had none. His father was a milkman, and Paul lived with his parents in a small duplex in a transitional area just at the edge of downtown Los Angeles. He had no flashy convertible in which to speed down palm-lined streets toward the Pacific beaches, and with his slight build and average height there was no hope he'd star athletically or financially in the field of sports. No, even then Fegen had a keen eye for sizing up situations, and he had to concede that prospects were slim for fulfilling his dream.

In fact, he felt lucky if he could get a girl just to kiss him. Girls didn't kiss on the first date, not nice girls, the kind of girls he liked, and that was fine. The trouble was that he didn't often get to the second date.

Nevertheless, he clung to his dream. He didn't want to be a pilot when he grew up. He didn't especially want to be a doctor, either. He didn't want to be President or a movie star. All he wanted was to be a lady's man. There were no courses in this, his chosen career, but he nevertheless enrolled at the University of California at Los Angeles and eventually settled into a job as an investigator for Dun and Bradstreet, the credit rating company.

The job taught him how a lot of businesses got going swiftly, then sprouted out in all directions, overreaching themselves and falling short of money, until they collapsed. It was dull work, but he was making $75 a week, had bought the mandatory automobile on the installment plan, and spent regularly on assembling the wardrobe he felt was required for his real vocation, the pursuit of gorgeous women.

"But you're not getting anywhere," his friend Connolly argued one summer weekend evening when they met in the stag line at a house party. "You've got no future."

"I'm earning a living," Fegen replied. "I go to parties at least once a week." After women, Fegen liked parties most, parties where there were—you guessed it—lots of beautiful women. Fegen liked and respected his college buddy Connolly, who was his best friend. Connolly had blond hair, a better tan than Fegen, and was considered smart. Fegen said, "Let's go get a glass of fruit juice."

The music was loud and everyone was dancing the new craze, the Twist. Fegen gaped hungrily at a blonde dancer in toreador pants who was moving with a maddening, controlled abandon. He suddenly realized his friend was talking.

"Why don't you go into law school, like me," Connolly was urging. "Then you'll get somewhere. You'll have a secure future, and you'll make a lot more money."

Fegen wasn't interested in making a lot more money.

Not that way. He had his used 1950 blue Plymouth convertible, even though the top was torn and he couldn't afford to fix it. On $325 a month, he barely had enough for clothes and dates, and he certainly had no desire to spend two more penurious years in school. Couldn't Connolly see that Fegen's ambition didn't require a degree in law? "I wouldn't pass the entrance test anyway," Fegen concluded.

But Connolly persisted. "You'd pass easily," he said. "Believe me. Look, the entrance exams are next week, and it only costs five bucks to take them. What have you got to lose?"

"Five bucks, that's what," said Fegen. That was enough money for a Friday night date. He added, "I'd just be throwing the money away." His eyes were beginning to roam again to the girls on the dance floor.

"If you were a lawyer," his friend pressed, "you wouldn't be standing around wondering if some chick would dance with you. If you were a lawyer, *they'd* be asking *you!*" That, you may be sure, got Fegen's attention. As a clincher, Connolly said, "Damn it, I'll give you the five bucks." He pulled out his wallet, took out a fiver, handed it to Fegen, and said, "Take the test."

Attorney Paul Fegen began looking for suitable offices in 1961, and in his accommodations as in his women, he knew exactly what he wanted. He wanted a suite, reasonable, at a good address, in a building with other lawyers, ideally with ready access to a basic law library. He'd be willing to share the services of a secretary-receptionist.

After months of legwork, looking for the right spot, Fegen decided it didn't exist. To get the good address, the first-class decor, and all the facilities he wanted, a beginning lawyer had to join a large, established firm in a very junior position, without even getting his name on the door. Otherwise, in the low price range he had in mind, the only offices available were gloomy closets in second-rate buildings with dirty windows and creaky, uncarpeted corridors upstairs above stores and banks. "If I had the money," Fegen thought, "I'd lease a whole floor in the right kind of building. I'd get together a whole bunch of lawyers who were looking for the same thing I was, and we'd all chip in on the rent."

Having no money, he compromised. He took a small, bare office alongside a half dozen other independent lawyers who also were just starting out. In the pursuit of his attorney's profession, Fegen developed a facility for getting promising cases—especially personal injury suits in automobile accidents. In fact, he attracted so much business that he began to let other lawyers down the hall do the actual work of building up a case and trying it, if it went that far. Fegen seldom appeared in court, but his name began to appear in the newspapers. He liked that.

In 1966, it all came together for Paul Fegen—his business background, his legal knowledge, his idea about the right kind of offices for lawyers. He'd never been satisfied with his suite, and he was always complaining, making constant suggestions to the man who held the lease.

"If you think you can run this place better," the landlord said in exasperation one day, "why don't you run it yourself?"

Fegen took over the lease, without the heavy investment that normally would be involved. He had been making a good living as an attorney, but suddenly he found himself making ten times that much by leasing and subleasing offices. His idea, creating first-class suites of offices, became so profitable, so quickly, that Fegen eyed a new bank building under construction on the fashionable Wilshire Boulevard in Beverly Hills.

He plunged. He leased the entire penthouse floor. He divided it up into luxurious offices, all for lawyers, charging them enough to make a fantastic profit. His suites followed a formula: luxury touches like expensive carpeting and paneling. A $70,000 law library on each floor. A conference room. Duplicating machines, telephone services, receptionists. Lawyers flocked to his doors. In the profession they began to call them "Fegen Suites."

The next year he took another floor in a new building across the street. Then two other floors, then four more. He couldn't afford to practice law anymore. Money was coming in from all directions as his idea swiftly grew into a multimillion-dollar business, one of the world's largest subleasing operations with a half million square feet of the most expensive real estate west of Arabia.

As landlord to a thousand lawyers, Fegen thrived. He blossomed. He fulfilled his dreams. Fegen instinctively knew that one of the basic requirements for the successful operation of luxury suites devoted to the practice of law is that the premises be peopled by beautiful young women: receptionists, switchboard operators, secretaries, file clerks, stenographers, typists, librarians, duplicating machine operators, office supply people, the personnel department, errand girls, girls, girls, girls.

Fegen took personal charge of hiring, surrounding himself and his lawyer tenants with the most beautiful girls in Los Angeles. One of the most common phrases overheard in a Fegen suite occurs when two lawyers, discussing a legal matter, take note of a Fegen beauty passing by in the course of her work: "Er, what was I saying?"

In the process of acquiring wealth and hiring beauty, the Fegen of teenaged fantasy emerged into real life. He grew a long, scraggly, hobo-type beard that lifted his average face out of the ordinary. He stood out in a crowd. He bought a $30,000 Excalibur sports car—open-topped, of course—and cruised the popular Sunset Strip with his trusty 200-pound black German Shepherd perched in the back seat like an elephant on a drum. And, with a special loudspeaker system rigged to his dashboard, he hailed the prettiest girls on the sidewalks, stopping to chat and invite them to his next party.

The parties are held regularly, most of them in his five-bedroom, five-bathroom house in the hills just above Sunset Boulevard, with a fantastic view of the city. The parties became so popular that fifteen policemen are required to block the streets and direct traffic. Pretty young girls have been caught climbing across rooftops trying to crash Fegen parties. Only 300 people are invited to the regular weekly Fegen party, on a ratio of two women for every man. Five hundred have to be turned away.

For occasional bigger parties, he rents a nightclub, a ballroom, or even the Hollywood Palladium, where 3,000 young people jam the building, 2,000 of the attractive young women personally invited by Fegen himself. He has met them all previously.

In his gigantic penthouse office Fegen keeps two Rollex files for parties, one listing women and the other men. The girls' cards contain a name, address, telephone number, and a personal note, like, "Barbara _____: fantastic body, likes to dance and swim. Met her in Malibu restaurant." Or, "Helen _____: short blonde, sensational face, bubbly personality. Introduced to her by Bob _____ at costume party."

Fegen has ways of getting attention. He will send one of his secretaries to the bank for hundreds of crisp new bills which he then sends to a printer to be made up into hundred-bill pads. Fegen then amuses himself, and others, by peeling off bills from the pads and giving them away. It's a sure-fire crowd-pleaser.

He likes to dress in wild costumes: in a silver jump suit and the goggles of a biplane pilot, as a clown, a space man, a Renaissance member of the king's court. He can juggle tennis balls and ride a unicycle. Once he threw a $35,000 party to celebrate his first haircut in ten years.

His bedroom, a spacious affair with dark wood and heavy beams that give it a Mediterranean ambience, has its own bar, television, and a push-button bed that does everything but fly. Music, lights, and all electronic conveniences of the house are controlled by button from the headboard. And into this room have stepped eagerly hundreds of the most beautiful young women in a city known for its beautiful young women.

"It's incredible, just incredible," said Fegen over breakfast in a dim café on a Beverly Hills thoroughfare. "For someone like me who remembers when girls didn't kiss on the first date. Now I say, 'Linda, what skin! Your body is just beautiful.

Take off your clothes and let me look at you.' And they do it. They just do it.

"You know what they say? I hear this from so many girls, gorgeous young things built to perfection, perfect face, they say, 'But why do you want *me*, Paul? You can have any girl you want.' And I tell them, 'Because you're so beautiful.'

"It's not true that I can have any girl I want, of course. There are a lot I can't have, and when that happens, it becomes a challenge, of course, but if I can't get her, it doesn't hurt my ego, because there are hundreds I can have.

"It's not the money. Girls don't like me for my money. You know, I'm over forty now. One night last week I was sitting with a girl at one of my parties at the house. She was eighteen and just stunning. She wanted to stay the night, but I was committed, so I pointed to a good-looking guy against the wall, a guy about 32 who's got as much money as I have, and I suggested she talk to him, but she said, 'Oh, he's too old for me!' I said, 'Well, you know I'm older than he is.' And she said, 'But you're Paul Fegen.'

"If a girl likes me for my money, I'm not offended. I like her for her body. Her beauty. Believe me, that's fair.

"You don't think about money when you have it. Not the way you think about it if you don't have it. I have this ring here, with a diamond. If a girl told me she liked it, I'd probably give it to her. It cost me $500, but if it will please her and I can just go out and buy another one, why not? I frequently give things away, because they don't mean that much to me.

"Money? I like to give it away. Throw it away. I enjoy it. It's surprising, but sometimes you can't give it away. If you offer some money to someone, they get suspicious. 'Why?'— they want to know, 'why?' Younger people react best. They say, 'Gee, thanks, that's awful nice of you.'

"I love young people. Especially women."

To a greater degree than millionaires whose fortunes arise from sources not of their own making, the suddenly rich who are able to take credit for their own achievements seem most capable of enjoying the fruit of their needs. When their ideas bring them wealth, it seems an extension and a vindication of their personality, and consequently, they seem more disposed to live out their fantasies.

"I did it." The big man spoke the words firmly into a battery of microphones one afternoon in the late 1960's, reciting as though from a speech he had been saving for the Academy Awards. Actually he was a film producer, and the accomplishment he referred to was the purchase and opening of the old Pickford Studios in Hollywood. Producer Robert Aldrich stated that day, in the heat and humor of glory, "I did it. All by myself. There's no one to thank. Nobody helped me. In fact, a lot of people stood in the way. I did it all by myself."

Obviously, the business coup seldom reaches such a level of personal achievement, and not all the winners are able to revel in the rewards of victory.

"Some people deal with professional prosperity and success very well," commented the psychiatrist Dr. Gilberg, "but their personal life and their problems are ignored in the process, which thrusts them into seeking one success after another. The next success, that's always the one that will do the trick, make them feel comfortable with themselves."

The pressures wealth exerts bring a different set of problems than those faced by the poor and middle class, and they can reach the point where they cancel out the benefits of riches and turn a life of luxury into a rat race.

One morning Charles Tobias was driving from his 37-room mansion to his luxurious offices in his silver-gray Rolls Royce. At age 39, Tobias was rich. An electronics wizard, he owned a factory that employed a thousand people. He had four Ferraris and other expensive sports cars, a hundred tailored suits, diamonds, an art collection, a yacht—everything a man could want.

He got caught in the morning rush hour traffic, as usual, edging along in the powerful vehicle from zero to ten miles an hour. On the way to the office that day he had to stop to talk to the loan committee at the Bank of America about borrowing $3 million for an expansion project, and the idea of the huge loan worried him. In the heavy traffic he turned off the air-conditioner so that the engine wouldn't overheat. Sweat began to bead on his forehead.

He had been working fifteen hours a day, five days a week, eight hours on Saturday and a half day Sunday. He was tired and discontented. He thought about the lonely dinners the servants laid out for himself and his wife at a table meant to accommodate eighteen. "Why am I doing this?" he asked himself. "What do I need this for?"

Almost automatically, his thoughts turned to his beautiful, 60-foot white ketch, the *Mar*, which floated idle in its slip in the marina. He hadn't even seen it for six months, he'd been so busy. He reached for the telephone beside the steering wheel and snatched up the receiver, trying to calm himself and reminding himself that he should have his blood pressure checked. He got his secretary on the telephone and told her to advise the bank that he wouldn't be there. "And tell everybody else," he added, "I quit."

He never went back to the office. Nor to his wife. Friends tried to talk some sense into him, warning him that he was literally throwing away millions of dollars. He went to his boat, and, ignoring the dockside protests of friends, he untied the ketch, one line after another, and set sail. That was in 1971. He spent five years cruising around the world, filming a documentary about his travels, doing what he wanted, then returned broke—but happy. "This is what I've wanted to do all my life," he said. "No wonder I wasn't happy. I wasn't doing what I wanted to do."

The dimly lit and run-down establishment at 315 Twenty-Third Street in Miami evoked none of the glamour of the city's fame. Its glass-paned exterior, cluttered with taped-on signs and haphazard lettering, signaled the classic type of

American eatery known as a "greasy spoon," and nothing on the interior argued otherwise.

Behind the smoky, reeking grill in the back stood Ollie Gleichenhaus, more than 60 years old, a roly-poly, paternal, transplanted New Yorker wearing eyeglasses, bermuda shorts, and a stained white apron, with athletic socks and sneakers on his feet.

Ollie had been in hamburgers a long, long time. He had had a little hamburger stand in Brooklyn on Ralph Avenue near Sutter, back when it had been little more than a prairie, and he had moved to Miami during the Depression in 1935, opening up his current operation. One thing Ollie had going for him, besides his love for people, was his pride in craftsmanship.

He considered himself the world's foremost authority on the history and construction of the hamburger. Starting back in the days when the hamburger cost ten cents, he had begun perfecting it, mixing in precise portions of 32 different spices and sealing them into the meat—only three burgers to the pound—over an open hearth fire. He boasted, "I make a dressing you could put it on a rug and eat it."

His greatest joy was to sit on the counter, serving some truck driver and warning: "Don't ask for catsup. Just eat it. Try it. Take one bite. If you don't think it's the greatest hamburger in the world, I won't even take your money. But you got no taste, you bum."

Ollie had been known to throw out people he didn't like, but these cases were rare, happening only if somebody insisted on catsup and disagreed with his political views, of which Ollie would say, "I was Archie Bunker before there was an Archie Bunker."

He took pride in the fact that people came from all over town to try his hamburger. Even chefs came to Ollie's, which didn't surprise him. He said: "This is the ultimate hamburger. There is no way to improve it. And one burger's an entire meal."

There was the time the electricity went off, and with the

fan out, the joint filled with smoke. "Ya'd think people'd run out into the streets," Ollie said. "Nobody moved. 'You're all crazy,' I tole 'em, and there I was makin' burgers by flashlight."

It was one of his finest hours. Build a better hamburger and the world will beat a path to your door.

One day a tall, well-dressed, distinguished-looking young man entered Ollie's and took a seat in a booth, ordering a burger. Ollie watched as the man took his first bite, savored the creation, and smiled. But when Ollie returned to his grill, the man ordered another. And then another. When the man ordered his fourth burger, Ollie's pride turned to amazement. He knew for an absolute fact that one burger was an entire meal. He confronted the glutton suspect at this table and asked, "Hey, Mac, what's with you?"

The man identified himself as John Y. Brown, who had recently sold out his holdings as the Kentucky Fried Chicken king. He told Ollie, "I want to buy your recipe."

"G'wan, ged outa here," Ollie responded, returning to his grill.

The young multimillionaire pursued, and as Ollie remembers it, the phrase "million dollars" was spoken. All Brown remembers is that he offered a lot of money and stock if Ollie would do for the Lums restaurant chain, which Brown had just purchased, what Colonel Sanders had done for Kentucky Fried Chicken.

Ollie swore he'd never leave his hamburger stand, but in the end he did. He gave Brown the recipe exclusively for Lums, signing the million-dollar contract. He had to close his Miami place and travel America promoting the "Ollieburger" dressed in an old-fashioned straw hat, red scarf, and apron. He was becoming the Colonel Sanders of hamburger.

Five years later, after returning to his Miami home from a Midwest publicity tour, Ollie talked about his life in 1977: "I've been traveling all over the country, and I love it. I just saw the Wabash River. Me, for the first time in my life, after a lifetime behind the hamburger grill. Everywhere I go, my picture's in the paper and people recognize me. I love it. Money can't buy that.

"I live in a nice apartment on Treasure Island with my wife and you can look right out at the ocean. When I travel I can't wait to get home, and when I'm home I can't wait for my next trip. I'm really enjoying myself.

"Money, sure, I'm comfortable. I've got stock and all that stuff, and I've got a twenty-year contract. I'm 66 and my health is good. I feel good. I enjoy life. What more could I want?

"I never thought I'd sell out to John Y., but he got to me, though. He really knows how to get to a guy. It wasn't the money. I told him, 'Money, who cares?'

"It's not that I didn't believe him, but a million dollars, who needs it? Look, I can only drive one car, right? I can only sleep in one bed, right? I don't drink. I don't gamble. What did I need it for? Believe me, I didn't need the money.

"See, I love people. For me, it was always a pleasure to go to work in the morning. I was making a good living. I had a feeling for my work. My hamburger is like a painting, and I enjoyed just watching people eat it.

"But when John Y. said, 'Ollie, I'll make you a general: You'll be General Ollie, bigger than Colonel Sanders,' well, I must have started to look interested. He musta known he had me. He said: 'I'll make you a celebrity. People will recognize you everywhere. They'll ask for your autograph.'

"Well, that was different. People asking me for autographs. I signed the contract. Being a celebrity, that's better than money."

6. The Celebrities

In the Hollenbeck Division Police Station, a modern, blue-tile building that clashed with the older adobe and brick structures in the crumbling Mexican-American ghetto of East Los Angeles, a plainclothes policeman struggled, tight-lipped, filling out another routine crime report, a burglary, printing the details on a standard form. His green eyes were stern and his mouth formed a straight line.

Under "Victim" he filled in a Spanish surname and grunted in disgust and sympathy. Some poor, hard-working slob making maybe seven grand a year if he's lucky, the kind of guy who has to save six months to buy a television set or a bike for his kid, and he gets ripped off of everything he owns by some lousy hype burglar.

The cop liked his job, especially since making detective rank, but there were times when it all seemed futile. The burglary he had to report was one of a hundred every month

139

in his area, and after the paperwork was done and filed, chances were that'd be the end of it.

Finishing the report, the cop threw it in a basket on the light oak desk in the big, fluorescent-lit room. He glanced at the report one last time before leaving. It was a printed form with numbered boxes, none of them providing enough room to say all the things that he wanted to say. Number 42 was "Motive or other reason for offense." He'd put in the usual answer, "Unknown" because there was no room to tell the whole truth.

On the wall on the west side of the room, at the top of a big notice board, hung a poster-size chart labeled "Top Ten Burglars—Hype." The cops knew who did the burglaries. Ninety percent of them were done by hypes—drug addicts—who'd haul off a television set or bike and sell it three blocks away for twenty bucks so they could buy a bag of heroin.

In the squad room, in their patrol cars, in the bars after work, the cops would talk about it.

"Jesus, we catch a paroled addict with his arms full of needle marks, but still we can't bust him. Have to catch him in the act of shooting the stuff."

" 'Why don't you cops stop all these burglaries?' the citizens always gripe. "We know one lousy little hype will commit thirty, forty jobs a month just to feed his habit, but we got to protect *his* rights."

"What about the rights of the poor people who are getting ripped off?" the plainclothes detective would always argue. "What about the cost, the misery, the fear?" He knew that once a family's home was broken into, they never felt secure and safe again.

Besides the official report, the cop had scrawled many things on small slips of paper, private things, notes to himself which he crammed into his shirt pocket to take home.

It wasn't the kind of information the official forms demanded, but rather the kind of thing that intrigued him. It was why he liked this dirty job in the first place. It was where things were happening. During the day he wrote down little things, the way a suspect's eyes moved when he answered a question, the way he licked his lips. The seriousness when people looked at his gun; or when he flashed his badge, number 178, to get their attention. He wrote down the little stories cops told each other, about crimes and crooks and getting laid. Once in a while another cop would ask him why he was taking notes and he would answer, "I'm writing a book." The other cop would give him a disbelieving look and say, "If it's none of my business, just say so."

But it was true about the book. When he got home every night to his small house in Walnut, a secluded suburb off the San Bernardino Freeway in the San Gabriel Valley east of the city, he never had much time with his wife Dee, a pretty, blue-eyed blonde, or their kids. He either had night school or there was writing to do.

He had taken a college class in creative writing and sent off a police story to *Atlantic Monthly*. It had been rejected, but in an encouraging way. "Dear Mr. Wambaugh," the editors had written, "You may have talent, but this kind of material might go better in the form of a novel."

So Joe Wambaugh began a novel. He was a disciplined man, able to organize his time and force himself to do work that was hard to do. He was a perfectionist, with a fine eye for detail, and he wrote about police work with all the love and hate that men usually heap on the memory of mistresses lost or disasters recalled.

Setting himself a pace of a thousand words a day, he allowed himself no excuses, pounding the pages out dutifully on a battered old Royal and having Dee retype the finished manuscript. He mailed out his book and it wasn't long before a publisher sent him a small check for it. But a big complication came up.

There was a rule in the Department that any cop who wrote any story for publication had to have it approved first by the high command, and even though this book was fiction, the Department, meaning the Chief, didn't like a lot of things that were said.

Which meant Wambaugh was in trouble, because he'd already spent most of the advance from the publisher, a mere $3,000. He knew that if he had to make a choice between police work and his book, there was no way he was going to give up a job he loved that paid $15,000 a year for a book that meant one little $3,000 check. As far as he was concerned, being a cop was not only the best job he'd ever had, but the highest paying. It was one of the reasons he'd joined the force.

"When I was a kid," he often joked, "I was so poor I thought the middle class was the upper class." He had grown up in a lowly suburb of Pittsburgh, Pennsylvania, joined the Marines, and married Dee, an eighteen-year-old telephone operator, right out of high school. He had worked in a steel mill before taking the Police Academy exam.

He wrote about his work because he cared so much about it. So it would be ironic if what he wrote cost him his job. No, if it came to that, the book would not get published. It was as simple as that. Somehow he'd have to pay back the three grand. Meanwhile, Wambaugh had some vacation time coming and needed a break, so he took his family on a one-week holiday in Mexico.

Returning home, he found in his mailbox a check for $38,000: the Book-of-the-Month Club had read his novel in galley form and wanted it. The next check was for $165,000 for the film rights. George C. Scott would star. And an even bigger check followed for paperback rights.

Meanwhile, the Chief of Police was persuaded that the book, *The New Centurions*, presented police work with a fresh, humanized look that would be good for the Department.

Said Wambaugh, "It all happened so fast you can't imagine."

His second book, *The Blue Knight*, which he'd nearly finished before selling the first, scored an even bigger success.

The checks were bigger, too. It was turned into a television series after William Holden played the lead in the film version. Then "Police Story" began on television with Wambaugh as story editor. Before the third book, *The Onion Field*, got into print, Joe Wambaugh was a millionaire.

Nevertheless, he stayed on the job as a cop. He was more than halfway to a twenty-year pension, and he was determined to stick it out. So every morning he got into his Cadillac and drove from his mansion in the rich old suburb of San Marino to the filthy barrio and its crime and violence.

Only four years ago, before he gave up his double life in frustration, Wambaugh tried to explain his love for the work. Taking a lunch break in an expensive restaurant-bar not far from the station, Wambaugh leaned forward, elbows on the table, squinting at faces in the place as though searching for suspicious characters. "Why do I still work as a cop?" he asked aloud, and answered, "Because for me being a cop is 'where it's at.' For me it is.

"If you ask my wife, I'm sure she'll tell you that it's much nicer being married to a writer than a cop. The kids, I think they're probably prouder of the fact that their father's a cop. They get sick of other kids asking questions about their dad's television show and the books.

"There are problems, trying to maintain this double life. I have to deal with agents, directors, all kinds of show business people as Joe Wambaugh the writer. There's one hard and fast rule I had to make: they can't call me at the police station. They're not allowed to bug me in my other life; that's my separate world. I don't have a private secretary. I work in a squad room with a bunch of other detectives and they get pretty annoyed with taking personal calls for me. Even my publicity agent has to call my wife, and I call her to pick up my messages. That's the only way the writer's world and the cop's come together."

The other cops didn't resent his other life, he said. "I'll tell you, I had to go to the firing range the other day to qualify for shooting, and a young patrolman stopped me and he told me he learned more about police work from my book than he had in all his experience on the force. Believe me, that was a good feeling. It was worth writing the book just for that."

What is it that makes him want to be a cop? Glamour? Danger? Is it so rewarding to chase crooks?

Wambaugh cursed quietly. "Police work is a holding action," he said. "That's all. Real police aren't as successful as those you see on television. We're not very successful at all. Most of the time you're doing your job after the fact—after the robbery, after the rape or theft, and if you catch any criminals, it's usually because some citizens gave you information.

"Danger? The physical dangers are overrated. I'm always fighting with 'Police Story' because they want to throw in gunfights and fist fights every four minutes, but in real life, well, I only fired my service revolver once in fourteen years on the force, and that was during the Watts riot. All of us were shooting at shadows then, just trying to stay alive.

"Emotionally, it's the most draining job there is. There's constant frustration. The better you do your job, the less you're liked, so you are performing your life's work without love. There's the odd hours, social and political problems, and a premature cynicism sets in."

Adding to the normal difficulty of the job for Wambaugh was the increasing problem of being a celebrity cop. Once he chased a suspect down an alley and collared the guy, spread-eagled him and read him his rights. When Wambaugh asked, "Do you understand your rights?" the suspect asked, "Hey, can I have your autograph?"

Things like that kept on happening. The last straw came one day when he answered an armed robbery call, a tavern heist. The holdup men had been vicious, pistol-whipping the bartender and customers before they fled. When Detective Wambaugh entered, the bartender, blood streaming from his head, struggled to him and said, "Tell me, what's George C. Scott really like?"

It was unreal. Wambaugh turned in his badge and gun

and tried to abandon his police life entirely, even though his best friends still were cops and ex-cops. The Wambaughs moved from the quiet San Marino suburb to the exclusive Newport Beach area. He tried tennis lessons. He tried boating, and still he felt like he was going "stir crazy." He started drinking a little too much. And he admitted he missed his work—the police work.

"I dream about it constantly," he said. "I'm only 40 years old and I've left an exciting life. I miss it." With a grin he added, "I think it's the lack of aggravation that disturbs me."

He admitted he had been appalled at the lack of integrity in Hollywood. He had fought the television and film executives at every turn, trying to keep them from corrupting his stories, as it seemed to him, with their injection of trite chase scenes, slugfests and shoot-outs. He'd ended up by suing, for a million dollars, the producers of the film which was based on his book *The Choir Boys*.

Disillusion with Hollywood had caused him to flee to Newport, California, but in the fall of 1977 he moved back to San Marino, into a different mansion, to resume his battle with the film people. To him, it was a matter of integrity. He was determined to produce the film version of his latest book *The Black Marble* himself, from his own script. From Joe Wambaugh, cop, to writer, to film producer.

Chances are he could show Hollywood how to do it right. He commented, "You have to throw your weight around and use more intimidation in Hollywood than I ever did as a cop. And it's a good idea to keep your ass against the wall, or somebody'll try to unscrew it and sell it.

"I'd rather tangle with a burglar than a television executive any day."

The celebrity is widely regarded as the epitome of The American Dream. Wealth, fame, talent; he's got everything, whether it's as a lionized writer, a film star, a "name" athlete or a gold-record musician.

Hollywood loves to tell publicity tales about how a stunning actor or spectacular performer became a star overnight, but the fact is that few have become stars without trying damned hard to get there and getting a lot of help along the way.

Without a doubt, television can and does make stars overnight. Actors and actresses who had been averaging less than a hundred dollars a week in pay can suddenly step into a role in a hit comedy or drama series and be catapulted instantaneously into the $5,000-a-week bracket.

Bill Macy, a middle-aged actor, was living in a $60-a-month room, often going hungry; then he signed a contract to play husband to "Maude" in the hit television comedy series of that name. Actor Carroll O'Connor sweated through a dozen years of film and television acting—none of it very profitable—before he was offered the role of Archie Bunker in "All in the Family" for $5,000 a week, a salary which through the seasons was extended by another zero. He observed:

"It may sound like a lot of money, but I remember when I first came out to Hollywood in '58 or '59, I wasn't making much. My wife had to go to work, and I was getting a television role here or there, and then nothing for months. Well, you average it out, and then figure that taxes keep sixty cents on the dollar, and it isn't exactly overnight wealth, is it?"

By contrast, comedian Jack Lemmon, after a long and distinguished career that began with his "overnight" fame from the role of Ensign Pulver in the post-war film, *Mister Roberts*, commented, "Nobody's worth what I'm paid."

Of course, the exorbitant salaries are paid because production companies strain for profits by buying the best possible ingredients, including talent, to make a show successful. Fame befalls the relatively unknown when budgets don't allow the top pay required by established stars. A performer in a new television series that succeeds quickly will predictably be mobbed by fans, in person and by mail. Mourned one producer, "Last year they couldn't earn $250 a week, and now suddenly they're not satisfied with $10,000. They want to become instant millionaires. They think it's *themselves* responsible for their success."

Indeed, television has proven that exposing even a relatively untalented *cat* to a mass audience will result in requests for its biography, which in the case of Morris, a feline appearing in commercials, was actually published.

During a strike of television newscasters several years ago, an executive who substituted himself for the "star" of the show found himself an instant celebrity.

Obviously, many talented performers earn a justified reward in their particular medium, but they often find in the process that they must share celebrityhood with others less deserving than themselves. Meanwhile, they know talented friends and colleagues who—like themselves until recently—remain uncelebrated and underpaid.

Television stardom may frequently be based more on exposure than talent (the demands of developing the latter explaining why so few *real* stars exist), but a TV star whose hair or physique has won popular acclaim often may feel almost compelled to prove that he or she is more than a media phenomenon, and this is an entirely understandable emotional need. Even film goddess Marilyn Monroe was tormented by the fear that it was her face or bottom that people loved, not herself. Such fears may have contributed to her tragic death.

When she was sixteen years old, the beautiful, dark-haired actress Susan Strasberg scored overnight fame and riches, her name shining in lights on Broadway as the star of the hit play, *The Diary of Anne Frank.* In the heat of this success she was brought to Hollywood at great expense and with much fanfare. "When I first came to Hollywood," she recalled years later, "I didn't really know what made me a success. You wonder what you've done that people think is so good; you secretly know that you weren't that good, and you're afraid maybe you're fooling somebody and they'll find out."

The manipulation of public opinion—which a phalanx

of agents, publicists, producers, and media executives handle masterfully in the interest of their percentages—confuses the very nature of celebrity status, inflating it out of all reasonable proportion and often bringing the bubble to the breaking point.

When Mark Spitz, the dashing young swimming hero, swept seven gold medals in the Olympics, he became an instant celebrity and immediately abandoned his amateur status. Yet he was so unaccustomed to money that he demanded his first payment, for a story about himself, be made in cash, in U.S. bills, and so $10,000 was delivered to his motel room. He spread it on his bed and reveled in it.

But Spitz saw his greatness as a swimmer somewhat overshadowed by the "media creation" type of celebrityhood that was rather violently imposed on his tender post-Olympic career. He had trained for years in anticipation of Olympic stardom, practicing daily, and preparing himself mentally to win, but he had not prepared for the resulting fame and wealth. "I couldn't handle it," he said recently, having since redirected his career toward more sports-related activities. "I just wasn't prepared for it."

Actress Sandy Duncan, who had danced since childhood and performed on Broadway before making a whirlwind rise to celebrity status thanks largely to an oft-repeated commercial promoting a bank, said: "A lot of people come to Hollywood and make it, and it turns their head, but that's silly. If you recognize what success like this is really all about, it doesn't bother you. The money? I don't think I have so much more. It just goes."

But the money that buys the accessories and visible signs of celebrity status is quite important. Actor Michael Caine, a handsome, blond personality who was propelled out of working class, cockney London by such film vehicles as *Zulu* and a series of spy thrillers to the point that he was eagerly sought as leading man for the most prominent actresses of the 1970's, commented, "It's funny how you adjust to having a few bob around.

"At first, whenever I bought something expensive, I'd be cool to all appearances, but before I got out of the shop my shirt would be sticking to me with sweat. Part of that remains. You never completely get used to it—success and money. You're amazed when it comes, amazed that it keeps coming, and, I suppose, amazed when it's all over.

"That's part of the price of success. You've got to keep looking over your shoulder and working like hell or you might slip.

"It wouldn't matter to me if it all ended just as suddenly. I was born poor and I could go back to it just like that. That's easy enough to say, though, because I've already made enough that I don't think I'd ever be poor again. I do think it would be awfully boring. Rich is nicer."

It can be glorious: Mary Wilson, who came from a housing project in the Detroit ghetto where her widowed mother worked as a maid to support the family, rose swiftly to stardom as a member of the original "Supremes," a top singing group of the 1960's. "One of the biggest thrills of making a lot of money fast was being able to do things for my mother, who worked so hard for us," said the singer. "I bought her a two-family duplex. I bought myself a Rolls Royce, lots of minks and foxes, a four-carat, heart-shaped diamond ring—and clothes, I just went crazy buying clothes." Her home now is a mansion in Los Angeles complete with a swimming pool and tennis court.

Actress Susan Blakely went from earning eighty cents an hour as a salesgirl in El Paso, Texas, to $60 an hour the first day she tried modeling. The tall, lean, blonde with the laughing blue eyes was a scared eighteen-year-old when she arrived in New York, but the first day she applied for work as a model the agency sent her on a commercial job. She couldn't even afford bus fare. But she worked hard, and her income climbed to a heady $100,000 yearly.

Dining in a chic Hollywood restaurant, after her hit success in TV's "Rich Man, Poor Man," she displayed an independent attitude that was part of the power of her money:

"After 'Rich Man, Poor Man' I had a choice of any series I wanted. But I told the producers, 'You can't offer me enough money.' I just didn't want another series. Money? I don't think twice about turning down incredible amounts of money if I feel a role is not right for me."

Some sudden celebrities never learn to enjoy the fruits of their status, unable to accept the loss of privacy, the demands on their time and person, the artificiality of mass approval, excessive income, and the power to gratify every desire. In the face of these sweeping changes from normal life—even though they were sought through a chosen career—one minor personality flaw can expand under the pressure and explode.

Psychiatrists observe that many entertainers—perhaps especially rock stars and musicians who work in the drug culture fringes—are liable to "freak out" attempting to anesthetize themselves from the problems of coping. Frequently the most devastating problem is the effort to reconcile one's own shaky self-image with mass approval. Such conflicts don't always result in drug abuse, naturally, but hints of unsatisfactory private life often appear in divorce and bankruptcy proceedings, gossip column revelations of extramarital affairs, news of "temperamental" outbursts, and frequent legal suits disputing contracts—all giving evidence that celebrities are not exempt from the human condition.

Actor Robert Blake, who went from a life of occasional film employment to $1.5 million a year as the offbeat television detective Baretta, only to experience the breakup of his family at the height of his success, observed, "Whenever you think you've got it made, Old Mother Nature gives you a kick and says, 'Hey, I'm still in charge.'"

Considering the way fame and sudden money can balloon a new star into a dangerous fantasy world, it's actually something of a minor miracle that any of them manage to keep their heads.

The accomplished character actor Jack Warden, whose durable career has spanned the rise and eclipse of dozens of other stars, replied thus when asked if it's the money that throws new celebrities off balance: "It depends. It's hard to take a young kid off the street and tell him to be careful. Be careful of what? Prior to that he was making $35 a week and now he's making a fortune, and be careful? This is the dream. It's not easy."

"Watch," one judge said to another. "She'll burst into tears."

"The winner will cry," said a spectator. "Why do they always cry?" Actually, though the crowd didn't know it, there was a very good reason for tears.

The room hushed as the master of ceremonies bent closer to the microphone, gesturing at the line of beautiful young women adorning the stage in frothy gowns, their smiles frozen on their perfect faces. "And now the winner," the emcee announced, "the new Miss Appleton, Wisconsin, 1972 . . ." He paused to assure that all attention was centered on his words, then in a strident voice boomed, "Terry Anne Meeuwsen!"

A statuesque, 22-year-old, brown-eyed brunette with a calendar-girl figure stepped forward gracefully to accept the title amid applause, music, and congratulations. Tears blurred her vision, but her smile radiated gratitude and she thanked everyone in a composed voice.

"I'm so proud," she told them, "I'm just delighted," she said, receiving all the hugs and kisses as if she really were completely happy.

Cry? She continued crying for two days. Whenever she was alone in the small, sparsely furnished room—a rocking chair, dresser, closet, and bed—the fix she had gotten herself into hit her, and the tears would flow down her beautiful cheeks.

Now that she'd won Miss Appleton, she was committed. But all her plans would come to a standstill if she got no further than the Miss Appleton contest. There was no money in that. It was such a risk that it might have been better if she'd lost; then at least everything would be settled. But she'd signed the entry blank, and much as she liked the little town of Appleton, she bristled at the thought of a whole year of making personal appearances at Chamber of Commerce meetings, clubs, and little parades.

She'd turned the course of her whole life around to pursue one specific goal, and now that she reigned as Miss Appleton, the biggest hurdles lay before her. When she was sitting there in that little room, so far from her goal, New York, it sometimes seemed absurd to have risked so much on such a distant chance, against so much competition from all over the country, when the only title that would mean anything in terms of her plans was the very top. And thousands of beautiful girls wanted that title.

Well, at least if she won the next step, Miss Wisconsin, she'd get to see more of her family and friends in her home town of De Pere. And there was a man named Tom Camburn whom she wanted to see more of.

But thoughts of romance were secondary to the realization of her overriding goal. To improve herself as a performer came first. She knew she was talented, but she also knew that there was a lot she had to learn. She wanted expert instruction, and there was no doubt in her mind where that kind of instruction could be found. And that's why she needed a lot of money, quickly, so she could afford to study singing, dancing, and acting in New York. If she won the Miss America Contest, she'd get thousands of dollars and a scholarship. But anything less than the very top prize would mean the end of the dream.

It wasn't a new thing, this dream of an exciting career. She had studied voice since childhood, and she knew that she had the face and figure of a star. After a year of college, she had made a stab at a singing career on her own, then had joined a large vocal group that traveled from city to city. But the pay was low and the recognition nil. She had been just another face in the chorus and her big break in show business had never materialized. So she'd returned after a while to her family's modest home in De Pere, Wisconsin, to decide what to do next.

The house was a middle-class, three-bedroom residence and she shared the whole upper floor with her younger sister. Terry had never felt that small-town life was too boring for her. In fact, the warm, secure, unruffled life her parents led appealed to her so much that she had often been torn between the idea of a career and the choice of most women: marrying, settling down, and raising a family. Back at home she worked occasionally, modeling or as a style show commentator, but she had a hard time making ends meet and couldn't even afford a car. But she still had ambition.

People who really knew show business had told her she simply had to go to New York and study full time if she really expected to get anywhere in show business, but that had been out of the question financially. Her parents had no money for that.

Then one day a friend suggested that she set her sights on the Miss America Pageant. After discussing the possibilities —the really long odds—with those closest to her, she had decided that at least she'd have a fighting chance.

Only after winning the first notch of her impossible dream did she realize how much she had riding on a very risky bet. She felt there were so many other girls more beautiful than she, maybe more poised and talented, and most of the contest entrants were younger—from eighteen to twenty-one. But fortunately, after winning the Miss Appleton banner, there was little time for self-doubt.

Days and weeks flew by in preparations for the Miss Wisconsin event, which she won, this time crying tears of unabashed joy and gratitude. Weeks later, she wept again as she stood on the traditional victory ramp in front of network television cameras, her arms full of flowers, the regal cape over her shoulders, scepter in hand and on her head the crown—of Miss America! She was, in fact, overcome with emotion as she realized that her dream, all of it, had come true.

"It all seemed so very strange to me," said Ms. Meeuwsen later. "One day I was living with my folks in De Pere, trying to make ends meet and to decide where I was going, and then suddenly the most amazing things were falling into my lap.

"Even before I won the Miss America competition people gave me thousands of dollars worth of clothes just so I'd wear them during the Pageant. It was a far cry from the times I couldn't even afford to shop at a department store, and always had to look for clothes that were on sale."

With all expenses paid during her reign, the money she earned for personal appearances and product endorsements began to pile up in her home-town bank. She spent a year on the road working almost seven days a week and sometimes up to twelve hours a day. The pace was so hectic that two women traded off working as her traveling companions. One would accompany her for a month and then take the next month off while the other did the job.

Ms. Meeuwsen earned more money than most reigning Miss Americas, in part because her inclination not to take sides on controversial issues resulted in many more bookings. At the end of her reign she'd amassed the queenly sum of $83,000, plus the $10,000 scholarship.

"All that money I earned so fast opened a whole new world to me," she recalled. "It was a very exciting, almost a Cinderella kind of feeling when I could go into any store and buy and not have to think about the money.

"I'd never had any real jewels or a fur coat before. After I won I went almost straight to the jewelry mart in New York and bought a beautiful diamond and ruby ring. In Indiana I bought a full-length mink and fox coat.

"I made my move to New York, after my reign was over. I was afraid being there alone, so it was important to me to live in as secure a place as possible. I rented an apartment where there was a doorman and an elevator man. It cost $400 a month for the one-bedroom apartment, but by the time you got through tipping everybody, it was a lot more expensive than that.

"It was a far cry from when I was traveling from city to city singing with a group. Then I couldn't afford to stay in a nice place when we appeared in New York. Everything was so expensive we looked for a place where we could pay as little as possible. We stayed in a hotel on 42nd Street near Times Square that was awful. There were prostitutes and all those weird people.

"It was a great expense just to set up a household. A friend took me to the Furniture Mart and it was a thrill to be able to go around the floor and say I'll take that, that and that and that.

"I signed up for lessons in acting, speech, voice, and dance. Though I could have continued earning money with a lot of personal appearances, I accepted few, because I wanted to concentrate on my studies.

"When I went anyplace I'd take a taxi instead of the subway. Even when I shopped for food I went to a nearby delicatessen instead of picking up groceries at a market a few blocks away, which would have been a lot cheaper.

"After about a year I got a phone call from an officer of my bank, calling to tell me I was going to have to take out a loan to pay my quarterly taxes. It was a shock to hear that my money had run out. I guess I didn't realize that money could go that fast. I just didn't watch it. I didn't know what my financial situation was from moment to moment during that year. I figured, you know, if it got dire, they would let me know. And I guess the people at the bank figured I would know exactly what was going on.

"It was a case of the right hand not knowing what the left was doing. I was in a tremendous tax bracket overnight and I just didn't understand my entire financial situation. I really blame myself for not keeping on top of it enough to know what was going on.

"After the shock of that phone call, I cut back on expenses immediately. I walked six or seven blocks each way carting groceries, took subways instead of cabs, and took on a lot more work to pay the bills.

"I was able to get only a few small roles in television series. It wasn't as intriguing as I thought it would be. There was a lot of waiting around in trailers for somebody to say, 'You're on.' And then you'd speak seven lines over and over again about fifteen times. I continued public appearances as a former Miss America, too."

By 1976 she had returned to Wisconsin, living in Mequon, a Milwaukee suburb, married to her faithful fiancé, Tom Camburn, who works in sales management. They enjoy a rustic life, sharing a rented 100-year-old converted fieldstone barn on 160 acres with their two dogs.

"I still do a lot of work that is a carry-over from being Miss America—speaking engagements, public relations work, and I sing at community concerts. My husband and I have written children's books together and I'm working on a book about how my life changed as a result of becoming a Christian several years ago. I'd still like to work in television some day, maybe with my own talk show."

As for how her celebrity experience as Miss America looks from a distance in time, she said: "What I really wanted was growth and confidence as a performer. All the money I made enabled me to devote myself to study, and really helped me. It was a good time for me to get my head together too.

"I still have some beautiful mementoes from all that money, like furniture, clothes, and jewelry. I really appreciate having them and I admire them. But the experience made me realize that if the other things in my life are the way they're supposed to be, I don't need all that to be happy. It's one of those things that you hear people say a lot, you read a lot, and maybe you even say it yourself. But until you've experienced the things I have, I guess it really doesn't sink in."

7. The Seekers

Raul Hurtado, his bronze skin baked by the tropical sun and his straight dark hair falling on his forehead, hurried along the rough sandy beach, squinting ahead to a rocky cove where his brother Francisco was to meet him. Occasionally he looked back over his shoulder. It was important that no one follow him on these walks, which he made daily now on the beach at El Bayjo del Rio de Medio, a clustering of fishermen's shacks two miles north of Veracruz on the gulf coast of Mexico.

Hurtado, who was 25 years old—a poor octopus fisherman with a wife and four children to support as well as his wife's impoverished family—knew little of the history of the shores he walked. He didn't know that the Spanish conqueror Cortez had landed his great ships and armored men there 450 years before in an invasion that had crushed the Aztec Empire of Montezuma, or that English, French, and American warships had assaulted the port of Veracruz through the years.

In his village, where the people survived on seafood and beans and where a hard-working man was lucky to earn a dollar a day, Hurtado had tried to make a living as a bricklayer, knowing how to construct homes from the local stones or concrete blocks. But he had nearly starved at that trade because nobody could afford to pay for such a luxury as a house of brick. So, like his brothers, Jesus, Roberto, and Francisco, he had turned to the sea.

Even with a small boat—and Hurtado could not afford even that—fishing was a hard life on those wind-raked shores where the seas were rough for nine months of the year. Having no boat, he and his brothers would wade and dive to explore the rocky inlets where octopuses gathered and could be taken in small nets or grabbed by hand.

Some days the fishing was good, especially during the summer, but it was always treacherous. The surf could pound you against the coarse rocks and scrape bloody patches from your body or limbs. The undercurrent threatened to sweep you out to sea. On days when the undertow was strong, the octopuses would be drawn out to deep water where sharks would find them, and the feeding sharks in large numbers would cut closer and closer in to the beach, devouring anything that moved. Meanwhile, the current stirred up the dirty sand bottom, clouding the water until you could see nothing.

During the later summer of 1975, under six feet of water in the rocky cove, Hurtado had found something strange on the bottom. It was a small length of yellow-brown metal shaped like an overstuffed sausage or a rounded bread loaf and weighing about two pounds. The surface had been worn smooth by the ocean but, examining the object in the sun, Raul had noted the letter "C" stamped in it. He had tried to guess if it might be a fragment from an old boat or chain, but the shape was not like any tool or fixture he could imagine. Still, it was a curious object and he had taken it home.

For several days the piece of metal, heavy as lead, had lain on the floor of his shack and the children had used it as a toy. But when a neighbor had seen the children playing with it, and expressed the belief that it might just be valuable, the Hurtado brothers had decided to take it to a Veracruz jeweler and see if, in fact, it was.

In the city, the first jeweler they visited had examined the object and said it was obviously just a piece of bronze weld, but the shopkeeper had offered to buy it for 150 pesos. Disappointed, but suspicious, the Hurtados had declined and left the store. Their suspicions seemed confirmed when the owner had followed them to the street and offered more money, which, from him at least, they had declined. They went instead to the shop of Luis Ortega, a respected jeweler on the Avenue Premiere de Mayo. Ortega had scratched at the bar with a small, sharp tool, examined it with an eyeglass, and weighed it. He had looked curiously at the "C" stamped in the metal. Then he'd offered Hurtado the fabulous sum of 11,000 pesos—the equivalent of $880—more than two years' earnings!

Hurtado had been overjoyed. Even if Ortega had told him the metal was pure 24-carat gold, it wouldn't have meant much to him. He had no idea of the price of gold on the world market. But with that much money, Hurtado had felt rich. He celebrated. He fixed the roof on his shack, bought a new bed for himself and his wife, and a stove. For a while the family had eaten well, much better than their jealous neighbors.

But the money had gone quickly. The winter seas had arrived, and even on calmer days when Hurtado risked searching the bottom of the rocky cove again, he could find no more of the valuable bars. He really didn't know if there were any more. But he knew he had to look. It was summer again and this day was the calmest since the past September when he had made his first find. He was eager to resume the search.

The gold of Montezuma has been the ultimate dream of treasure hunters since the 1500's, and much has long been known about it, authenticated by experts in the archives of Seville, Spain. Pages and pages of old handwritten ship manifests list the cargo of treasure vessels item by item, describing bars of gold stamped with the imperial "C" for Carlos, King of Spain, and Emperor of the Holy Roman Empire—which included most of Europe. The standing order to his world-roving armies and navies was simple: to capture gold, melt it into bars, and bring it to him directly. With it he financed his wars, kept the peasants in line and carried out the bloody Inquisition.

Tons of gold and silver bullion, coins minted by favor-seeking colonial officials, and fine jewelry taken from the Aztecs had been loaded aboard a fleet of twenty Spanish ships at Veracruz in 1553. Creaking under their burden, the ships had sailed into a hurricane and suffered total destruction. It was told through an eyewitness account that half of the ships were battered to pieces in the surf off the Gulf of Mexico at the lowest point of Texas. Three hundred survivors, including wealthy merchants and their ladies, made their way ashore at Padre Island only to be slaughtered by Indians. Two men escaped, however, one a sailor and one a priest; the latter led the earliest salvage expedition, but with little success.

The sailor, who was captured by Indians and who lived with them the rest of his life, may be the originator of the first of the hundreds of lost treasure maps, real and bogus, which have been available to travelers at a wide range of prices for centuries. As Cortez himself believed, and as the legends repeat, the bulk of Montezuma's treasure was never captured by the Europeans. Gold and silver had been carried north at the Aztec emperor's orders, away from the advancing Castilian armies, and buried in caves in what is now Arizona or New Mexico. Or the treasure was taken south and hidden in old temples. Many maps were marked with the magical X. The number of charts that showed where the ships had been wrecked multiplied.

But for 400 years, nothing.

In the classic film, *The Treasure of Sierra Madre* (Warner Brothers, 1948; directed by John Huston from a book by B.

Traven), Howard, the old prospector in the Tampico flophouse, is overheard expounding on why gold is so valuable:

> Howard: *A thousand men, say, go searching for gold. After six months, one of 'em is lucky—one out of the thousand. His find represents not only his own labor but that of the nine hundred and ninety-nine others to boot. Six thousand months or fifty years of scrabbling over mountains, going hungry and thirsty. An ounce of gold, mister, is worth what it is because of the human labor that went into the finding and getting of it.*

One of the thousands of men who pored over maps of the Montezuma treasure down through the ages—the sea-borne and the buried portions—was a tall, wiry, balding ex-chicken farmer destined to become one of America's best-known adventurers. His name was Melvin Fisher, and he had successively, over the years, deserted the Midwest for California, abandoned chicken farming for engineering, and quit engineering in order to open a diving shop at Redondo Beach, California, where he sold scuba equipment and boat gear.

Fisher's expertise in diving led naturally to a hobby of treasure hunting. It's a pursuit whose enthusiasts divide into two camps, the seekers of sunken treasure and the seekers of buried treasure. But Fisher, a tanned, genial, perennial optimist, at first tackled both. One journey took him to the sacrificial temples in the Yucatan jungles of Mexico, which had been under the reign of Montezuma. But no legendary hoard was discovered.

In 1963 Fisher sold out his diving shop and joined with a group of similar-minded individualists who believed that fortunes awaited them at the bottom of the sea. Their plan was to carry out their quest all around the coastal waters of America, but especially near Florida, in the shipping lanes where, centuries before hurricane warnings, the Spanish had ruled the seas.

To Fisher and his friends, this was no wild adventure. The fact is that since World War II, salvage methods had made revolutionary advances, and many of them had not yet been applied to treasure hunting. And now, suddenly, the discovery of sunken wrecks was no longer an entirely hit-or-miss affair: The Archives of Seville, Spain, had recently yielded long-lost and highly detailed charts, journals, and sailing orders of many sunken ships and their cargoes. The promised rewards staggered the imagination: according to official documents, an estimated $15 billion in gold and silver had gone to the bottom of the sea over the centuries, most of it in ships of the Spanish treasure fleet.

Fisher's new venture especially excited him because he had been trying to invent a device which could be used on the sea bottom to blow away the accumulated sand that usually hid the spoils of sunken ships, one of the biggest obstacles in hunting sunken treasure. His was a highly skilled trade, requiring not only diving expertise but a major investment in support ships and technical gear—including a new device, the magnetometer, which detected underwater metal. The old wood of the galleons never survived the centuries in salt water, but iron from anchors, ships' fittings, and cannons would betray their location. Still, when he set out on the new enterprise, moving with his wife Dolores and their young children to Key West, Florida, he decided that if he found no treasure after one year of searching, that would be the end of it.

Five days short of that mark, with nothing taken from the sea more valuable than a fish, the newly perfected underwater blower began operating as usual, and Fisher as usual watched the sand of centuries being swept aside. What happened next was anything but usual. Suddenly a glint of gold appeared on the bottom, then a virtual carpet of gold coins. Two thousand of them were brought to the surface in two days, some of them fabulously rare Royal doubloons which, when they went up for sale before frenzied collectors, brought prices of up to $25,000 for a single coin! It was a dream come true.

Fisher might have quit then. But in the same year, at the dry research library of the Smithsonian Institute, a 300-year-old list of ships was deciphered with the word "Atocha" at the very top, along with some incredible figures. "Atocha" it proved, was the name of a ship, and soon, piece by piece, research developed further facts about the long-forgotten *Atocha*. In 1622 the *Atocha* and her sister ship the *Margarita*, caught in a Caribbean hurricane, had been tossed onto reefs in the Matecumbe Keys off Florida, sinking in shallow water. The *Atocha* alone carried fifty tons of gold and silver, which perhaps explained why it topped what had proved to be a list of lost ships and their cargo.

"Six hundred million dollars, conservatively," proclaimed Fisher, after evaluating the *Atocha* records. And, he vowed, with his expertise, his knowledge of the local waters, and his equipment, he would be the man to find it.

The Archives of Seville yielded yet further data. The ship, the records said, had struck a reef and had sunk with its mast half exposed. The Spanish had sent salvage crews, tapping all known resources at the time, including a crude diving bell, imported pearl-diving natives from far islands, grappling hooks and chains. Another hurricane had crushed the first expedition and scattered the *Atocha* wreckage, but for 58 years the salvage attempts had continued fruitlessly at a terrible cost in lives and hardship.

Throughout the 1960's, many a treasure-hunting operation in America, great and small, swept the Florida Keys in search of the grand prize, the *Atocha*. All were convinced that, with "inside information," experience, or just sheer luck, the treasure would be theirs.

As it developed, it was no lusty seaman who proved the key to locating the treasure ship's wreck, but rather a scholar, a doctoral candidate at a Florida university whom Fisher sent abroad to recheck the Spanish archives. Numerous errors that the scholar detected in the old handwritten documents, including confusion about old place names that had been changed in a later century, led to a new and far more accurate picture of where the *Atocha* had probably gone down.

Fisher, his resources drained by the huge costs of the project—including the decrepit galleon replica he used as an office, the houseboat he lived in, a barge for the magnetometer, two 60-foot diving-support ships, and the costs of equipment, maintenance, divers, crewmen, and living expenses—resumed the search with new vigor once he had the new information. Back and forth he cruised the Marquesa Keys, looking for reefs which, in water neither too deep nor too shallow, could have snagged the *Atocha* and still left its mast exposed. Fisher knew that the ship would have split its bottom on the reefs, the cargo spilling and spreading in subsequent storms, but he knew as well that such a reef would be as good as an X marking the spot.

Every day, at a reef that seemed a likely prospect, Fisher's magnetometer boat crossed and recrossed, signaling objects below, and the divers found them: a wrecked target ship the Navy had shot to pieces, unexploded torpedoes, crashed airplanes, deadly mines, coiled steel cable, and oil drums. But the only discovery smacking of antiquity was the remains of a vessel dating no further back than the Civil War.

Treasure hunters, being dreamers, tend like their dreams to gloss over details. The vision always focuses on and revels in one isolated moment: the hero striding into a cave or swimming to the bottom and beholding there the dazzling sight of huge chests brimming with gold and precious jewels. Forgotten are the countless hours, days, and even years of arduous, frustrating search, whether by land or sea, the punishing labor of digging or diving until the body aches, and Nature's lack of neatness with the property men have lost.

Fisher, on the contrary, found his *El Dorado* under the depths an inch at a time. It began slowly in 1971 with the initial discovery of a musket ball that could have been aboard any seventeenth-century Spanish galleon. It proved nothing, but somehow Fisher *knew*. Then a coin was found, a giant anchor, an eight-foot gold chain, articles of exquisite tableware.

The search continued. Months passed. Years passed. The divers descended daily. Still, the underwater site yielded nothing that might not have been aboard any of dozens of different ships that had sailed the Caribbean in that era and met a fate similar to the *Atocha*'s.

In little victories occurring once every few months, a cache of thousands of small coins was recovered: a gold chalice embedded with emeralds, items of fine jewelry, an antique navigation instrument, small gold bars, and nearly a dozen bronze cannons of the type that armed the *Atocha*. These treasures, most of them sold to finance further exploration, however, were not among the items mentioned in the official documents.

Then, in 1975, paydirt! A large single bar of silver was recovered that weighed nearly 70 pounds! It had been etched with a number. Flipping frantically through his lists describing the nearly 200 such bars in the *Atocha* cargo hold, Fisher found it: the same number, the very same weight. Fisher let out a cheer and all the divers and crewmen joined in. They screamed for joy, drank, laughed, and celebrated. All doubt had vanished now. They had found it, verified it. A treasure of 50 tons of gold and silver, some of it worth a hundred times its weight because of its antiquity, lay waiting to be picked up.

This fantastic quest, uncovering one of the largest lost treasures known on the globe, had been brought to victory through the skill, inventiveness, tenacity, and hard work of the man who stood to profit most from the booty. It was beautiful. A dream come true.

But the dream soon turned to nightmare. Later the same month, Fisher's oldest son, Dirk, aged 21, was sleeping with his young wife aboard one of the diving ships which served double duty as quarters for crew members. The antiquated, overworked boat, a converted tug, sprang a sudden leak in the dark of night, flooded with water, rolled and sank without warning. Dirk Fisher, his wife, and another crewman drowned below decks.

As the days passed, Fisher, who had set out treasure

hunting when he was 42 and was 53 at the time he established the sensational *Atocha* find, took $6 million in treasure from the wreck, averaging a million a year from 1971 on, although the bulk of the tantalizing cargo still eluded him.

From these facts and figures, it would appear that Fisher had achieved his goal and that with tragic reason to be disillusioned with the sea, he could have retired as a multimillionaire, living a life of luxury and catering to his thirst for adventure by traveling the whole wide world.

But Fisher, having established a pattern of pursuing a dream over more than a dozen years, clung to it, optimistic that more than 300 loaf-like bars of gold and silver could yet be found where the *Atocha* once lay in the treacherous sea. The laws of salvage, moreover, required him to stay and work his claim, or abandon it to others. So he was obliged to act out his drama to the bitter end, until the last bar of gold, mined and molded by the enslaved of other worlds and other times, could be brought to the surface.

The task could continue to 1980, or even 1990. Meanwhile, Fisher insists that the treasure has not made him rich. To keep the operation going, he had been forced to promise shares to investors, so that dozens of people are now dividing the "loot." He has also been beset by legal battles with the state of Florida and the United States government, both of which have laid claim to his discovery. The costs of lawyers, the income tax, the 25 percent that Florida rakes off the top, the millions spent on wages and equipment, seem to dissipate any riches as fast as they are brought ashore.

The spectacular treasure hunter Fisher continues to live in a shabby Key West houseboat, a floating shack that might be condemned if it sat on dry land. He drives an old, battered car and tries to comfort his wife, who has been strong enough and willing to follow the dreamer in a life of uncertainty and insecurity. But she bears with difficulty the tragedy that befell them along the way. To her it doesn't balance out: A treasure won, lives lost.

As Christmas 1977 passed, the Fishers, cheered by a

partial release of confiscated gold by the government, figured
that at least they were better off than two years before, when
they couldn't even afford desperately-needed equipment. But
a final irony emerged. In much the same way that the gold of
The Treasure of Sierra Madre was swept by a windstorm back to
its mountain, the *Atocha's* gold now seems destined to complete the last leg of its originally intended journey to Spain: A
Catholic organization, having acquired the treasures Fisher
recovered, is planning to send them to the Prado museum in
Spain to honor the king, Juan Carlos. So, from the steaming
jungles of the Caribbean, the gold may finally make its trip
across the sea.

As for Fisher, he is philosophical about the deadly
power of the unfeeling sea, whose fury had sent the *Atocha* to
the bottom so long ago. He ponders the irony of a set of
circumstances through which a disaster at sea in 1622 had
spanned the ages to claim additional victims 350 years later.
The money? It was never the money, really, or if it was at first,
the hunger for gold had long since been eroded by time and
the sea. Fisher goes on with his work.

What makes a man set out in search of gold, flying into the
face of staggering odds, ignoring histories of failure and undaunted by the certainty of exhausting work? People unafraid
of hard work know that the economic system practically
guarantees them the equivalent of gold, meted out weekly in
small but sustaining amounts, if they will devote their time
and labor in regular continuing periods to causes that enrich
and serve others rather than themselves.

Of course, the workaday life, if it feeds the body, may
not nourish the soul, and many who are discontented with job
routines that provide some security but little future and less
food for the spirit dream of achieving sudden riches through
the discovery of sunken or buried treasure. Today, sea salvage for the most part excludes all but the professional treasure hunter. But the lure of buried gold and hidden money

beckons a veritable army of land-based dreamers equipped with no more than a metal detector, a shovel, and hope.

Does hidden treasure exist? Even apart from the legendary hordes of pirates, bandits, prospectors, and misers, a Federal Reserve Bank executive in Boston estimated in 1977 that Americans may have stashed away more than $50 billion in their own secret hiding places to avoid banks, their mates, the law, or the Internal Revenue Service. When events such as death, illness, imprisonment, surveillance, or senility prevent the owner from recovering his or her own cache, the money is often "finders-keepers." During the Depression, when banks all over America failed, people who had cash were stuffing it into bottles and cans and burying it on farms, inside walls, in attics or cellars.

From farther back, the storied hoards of history have become so widely known that the United States government, through the Congressional Library, publishes "A Descriptive List of Treasure Maps and Charts," available from the Superintendent of Documents in Washington for fifty cents and serving as a guidebook to hundreds of lost treasures with varying degrees of authentication.

Experts estimate that Americans unearth approximately $25 million in such buried treasure annually, much of it found by amateurs aided by sophisticated new equipment and detailed research which previously had been left undone. In land-based treasure, too, it has only been in the last decade or so that metal detectors have improved so much that people are scrambling over every hill where treasure-laden souls may once have roved, scanning for gold and coin that others sought in vain without the proper tools—and they are finding more than ever before.

When Bob Ellithorpe of Del Norte in lower Colorado was hired in October 1975 to bulldoze property near the ghost town of Summitville—a big mining region until World War II—he stopped to assist a pickup truck stalled at the roadside. Sitting beside the road, ten feet away, a craggy boulder of irregular shape, measuring about one foot high and two feet long, caught his eye. The rock had probably fallen off a truck and sat there in the sunlight for thirty years while thousands of people rode by. The rock, which weighed 140 pounds, proved to contain almost one-fourth solid gold and to be worth $50,000. The largest single specimen ever found in the state, it was eventually placed in Denver's Museum of Natural History.

In a transitional section of Los Angeles, which had been occupied in turn by generations of Jewish families, Mexican-Americans, and blacks, a small old adobe house that a dozen different families had rented (and where there must have been more than a few crises caused by a lack of money to buy food and pay bills) yielded a cache of $12,000 in 40-year-old bills and coins that had been crammed into jars and tobacco tins and hidden between wall studs.

A salesman's widow in Woonsocket, Rhode Island, discovered in 1965 that her late husband had created a secret chamber six feet wide under a small shed in their back yard. It was stacked nearly two feet high with silver coins, more than two tons of them, worth over $50,000.

There are small treasures and large ones, but, depending on how rich or poor a person happens to be, even a five-figure windfall can sometimes look like one of those legendary caves which maharajas filled with gold and gems.

Perhaps, in your very own backyard . . .

New Mexico's most barren land stretches from Las Cruces on the south to the old Route 66 on the north, a vast expanse of dead earth roamed at various times by Cochise and Billy the Kid, Pancho Villa and the U.S. Cavalry—hundreds of square miles of rock and sand that in thirty years since 1945 have exploded with the first atomic bomb, captured German V-2's, and a succession of rockets and other military hardware developed for the Army and Air Force. In this territory, a government reservation called the White Sands Proving Grounds, stands a small mountain called Victorio Peak. In a

District Court in Kansas in the 1960's a sealed file was registered as evidence which contained an inventory detailing the
alleged contents of a cave in Victorio Peak: a cache of gold
bars stacked like cordwood, varying in weight but totaling an
astounding 39,000 pounds.

At least one report hinted that Karl Von Mueller of
Weeping Water, Nebraska, recognized as one of the foremost
authorities on American treasure troves, author of *The Treasure Hunter's Manual* and a man of unquestioned integrity,
had performed the inventory in person. Others, including
former military personnel and neighboring ranchers, filed
affidavits swearing they, too, had seen gold at Victorio Peak.
Yet when the noted attorney F. Lee Bailey, after years of
fighting red tape, cleared the way for an expedition to Victorio Peak in 1977, its chambers were found to be empty.

Of course, hundreds of people had access to the site in
the 1960's and 1970's: soldiers, explosives experts who
periodically removed the "live" fallen munitions, mustang
scouts, nearby ranchers pursuing workhorses that wild mus-
tangs had lured away, and any other intruder foolhardy
enough to brave a desolate region scattered with unexploded
rockets and bombs.

Little doubt exists that the treasure was indeed once
there, but knowledge of its origin and disappearance remains limited to speculation until such time as those who
know the truth reveal the story. Some talk of the gold having
been hidden there by mission priests. Others say it was buried
there when a wagon train came under attack by Geronimo's
Indian army. Another story reports that it was part of a Con-
federate Army shipment lost at the end of the Civil War. No,
say others, Victorio Peak was the storehouse for old Spanish
mining operations. The name Montezuma occasionally comes
up. The most modern tale, completely lacking in documenta-
tion if not in drama, purports that the gold was flown to
White Sands at the same time the captured German rockets
were brought there under the cloak of the latter's Top Secret

coverage, that the gold was part of Hitler's national treasury, that it had been hidden at White Sands by conspiring military men and had been removed when treasure hunters began threatening an expedition.

Three thousand miles to the northeast, at Oak Island, Nova Scotia, a mysterious, wood-lined shaft leading to a series of interlocking tunnels, underground chambers and caves, was discovered in the 1700's and identified as similar to Caribbean island "pirate banks" which roving raider ships used to hide their captured loot on land. There is talk of Spanish gold ships, too. And, indeed, for what other purpose would anyone create such a complex network of tunnels, protected from intruders by more defenses than a modern bank vault, than to hide an extraordinary treasure?

But nobody—and fifteen expeditions have tried—has ever been able to get to the bottom of the mystery. The efforts of a Florida construction executive, Daniel Blankenship, who quit his job at the age of 42 to lead the latest expedition to Oak Island, have been fruitless after twelve years of effort and expenditure of nearly a million dollars. "I'm positive there's treasure buried there," he says. "But it's not the money I care about. It's the challenge."

The expert Von Mueller, in his *Treasure Hunter's Manual*, wrote: "There is very little likelihood that there is a county or parish in the United States that does not have several good treasure caches waiting for the first taker. . . . There are so many large, medium and small treasure caches located throughout the country that it seems almost inconceivable that more people do not find them."

If such a situation exists, why are we all just working for a living? Why aren't we out hunting treasure? There are reasons.

The professionals go after the biggest hoards and, with their expertise, often find them. That leaves only the smaller caches for the beginners, whose ranks are kept thin by the need to earn a living until one *succeeds*—and *big*—at treasure hunting.

And can you imagine writing on an employment application, under "Job History," the information that for the past two years you have been hunting for the fabled Bald Eagle Goldmine in Southwest deserts at a salary of zero? One man who did so had previously been a successful, college-trained executive. He realized, after his treasure-hunting stint, that he had burned all his bridges and was now virtually unemployable.

But the greatest barrier to a "career" in treasure hunting lies in the nature of the calling itself.

More than anything else, the treasure hunter is an adventurer. When an ordinary person's life becomes boring, which happens to almost everyone occasionally, one longs for excitement, something different, an adventure. But when that urge strikes, most people merely pack up and take a vacation, engage in a love affair, go on a shopping spree, yell at the kids, or seek some other rather conventional outlet. Few are daring enough to embark on true adventure in distant places.

Although the goal might seem to be riches, the comfort and luxury money buys, treasure hunting seldom appeals to anyone not inclined to physical activity and the outdoors— roughing it in the wilds of land or sea. To have even a chance of success, moreover, the would-be treasure hunter must also spend long hours poring over books and documents in the tamer surroundings of research libraries. Most people balk at one or the other, and the lost gold mine, or the buried treasure, continues undisturbed.

Anybody who is studious enough to do difficult research, is willing and able to endure hard work, is sharp enough to play detective with clues that have baffled others, and has a pronounced gambling streak, is usually astute enough to recognize how crazy it would be to hunt treasure for a living. So most potential professional treasure hunters find other avenues of private enterprise to pursue. Then, if they get bored after they get rich, they can always give treasure hunting a try.

Take, for example, two brothers named Paul and Max Zinica, who operated a successful ice cream factory in Gary, Indiana. Wearying of their profitable business in the late 1960's, they cashed in their equity and packed up to go treasure hunting. No starry-eyed, inept amateurs, they had read of a disaster at Padre Island off Texas in which ships of the Spanish fleet, carrying some of Montezuma's Aztec gold, had been dashed and sunk by a hurricane. To recover that sunken treasure became their goal.

They prepared expertly for their sea hunt, and their labors were soon richly rewarded. At a 100-mile long barrier reef barely three miles wide, a new causeway had opened up the strand of grassy dunes to tourist trade amid a minor boom of motels and resorts. On the beaches, shell-hunters had soon begun finding silver coins. Cruising off-shore in 1967, the Zinicas quickly located the source of the coins: the remains of a galleon with a cache of silver worth more than a half million dollars! But as quickly as they had found their treasure, the Zinicas' good fortune ran out when the state of Texas heard about their find and itself plunged into the treasure-hunting business. Texas hired its own divers and engaged researchers to probe Spanish archives for clues to the location of the rest of the Padre Island treasure.

The state-sponsored expeditions that followed, led by marine archeologists, pinpointed the wreckage of not one but three Spanish treasure ships off Padre Island, and the divers who were sent down brought up silver bullion, coins and discs, gold, cannons and cannon balls, marine instruments, crossbows, crucifixes and other jewelry whose total value far exceeded that of the Zinicas' finds. Next, armed with legislation called the Texas Antiquities Act, which (by some curious logic) empowered the state's Land Office to control its seas, state officials went after the booty discovered and removed by the men from Indiana. The treasure which the Zinicas, through their own initiative and industry, had found and recovered from the seas, was confiscated by the state of Texas. Ten years later it remained in a legal limbo, pending court appeals.

For the professionals who seek the treasure of Montezuma with the latest in magnetometers, underwater search equipment, expert divers, historical research, and large investments in ships and crews, it is perhaps disconcerting to see some unskilled person not even engaged in the quest, bump into a bonanza of gold that for years had been the experts' Holy Grail. But such can, and does, occasionally happen. Let's return now to Raul Hurtado, the octopus fisherman we met earlier in the chapter.

Hurrying along the beach at El Bajo del Rio de Medio, near Veracruz, Raul saw his brother Francisco waiting for him at the rocky cove. Francisco was waving and smiling, signaling happily that the waters were smooth and unmudddied for the first time in all of 1976.

They waded into the water together and took turns diving. One man always remaining on the surface to watch for sharks. During nine months of waiting for calm and clear waters, the brothers had planned exactly how they must search for more gold bars like the one Hurtado had found before, and they systematically sifted by hand tiny portions of the bottom, inch by inch, careful not to miss a spot.

Again and again for hours they took turns, one of them standing with only his head out of the water to rest a moment while the other dived. Raul came up spluttering water, trying to smile and talk and catch his breath all at the same time. "I found them!" he stammered.

"Them? How many?"

"I don't know. A lot, maybe."

One by one they brought up from six feet of water a total of sixty bars of solid 24-carat gold, plus sixteen other objects, necklaces and ornaments of the same metal. At the same rate at which he paid for the first bar, the jeweler Ortega paid the Hurtado brothers, who all pitched in on the big job of transporting the gold to Veracruz. The total came to 60,000 pesos, which to them was a fortune of stunning dimensions, though the equivalent of only 5,000 U.S. dollars.

In the Hurtado family there was unrestrained joy. The celebrating began immediately. There were gifts for all. Beer and tequila flowed and a feast was prepared, with the first meat on the table in a long time. One of the brothers took thousands of pesos and left on a spree with his girlfriend, visiting luxurious resorts all over Mexico, spending freely. A few days later, another brother disappeared with his share of the booty.

Raul Hurtado couldn't have been happier. He was glad to share the money with his brothers. There was plenty for all, so much in fact that he could now fulfill a long-held dream by building a concrete block house for his wife and children, right at his same address, Lote 19, Colonia Playa. He set to work at the task, enjoying every moment of it.

They tried to be careful about the neighbors and not to talk too much about their fortune from the sea. After all, more of the gold remained out there on the bottom. They had left it because they already had enough, but someday they might want more, and it would thus be kept in the family.

But the neighbors, still living in grinding poverty, stared and seethed at the splendid concrete house that Raul Hurtado had constructed. They saw the bottles of expensive liquor carried into the house. At the markets the Hurtados were observed buying the best food. In the Veracruz shops they spent like tourists, and back home the village buzzed with talk about the family.

Eventually, and inevitably, leaks sprang in the Hurtado family itself that broke their bond of secrecy, and soon it seemed everyone knew the general details of how the Hurtados had discovered their fortune. Word reached minor clerks and the officials in Veracruz who were their bosses.

And soon, the whole matter was reported to the national police in Veracruz.

Finally, in the fall, a year after his initial discovery of one gold bar, Raul Hurtado's brief experience with wealth and happiness came to a disastrous end, with police hammering on his door in the night, arresting him and his wife, and taking them away. Dragged before a magistrate in Veracruz, Hurtado was ordered to tell his story, and when he did, they summoned the jeweler Luis Ortega to verify it. He too was placed under arrest. The magistrate asked them both gruffly, "Didn't you know that the government forbids the plunder of Mexico's archeological treasures?"

It was no treasure, Hurtado pleaded. All it was was gold out in the ocean. "Archeological treasure?" What was that? "I didn't rob jewels from a museum," he protested. "The pieces of gold were at the bottom of the sea and belonged to no one. Except to me, who discovered them."

"But what about the jewelry, then?" the magistrate demanded.

Ortega answered. "It was in such bad condition that I never imagined the pieces might be of archeological interest." As for the gold, he declared, "My business is buying gold, and that is what Hurtado took to me. I committed no crime to buy it."

Warning that both of them could be sentenced to prison for up to ten years, the magistrate ordered them both locked in jail to await their trial.

All of the gold bars were recovered and confiscated by the police, as well as the objects of filagreed and laminated ornamental jewelry, also of gold, finely handcrafted. When the treasure was taken to the Veracruz branch of the Banco de Mexico, the director of the local university's Anthropology and History Institute examined the pieces and gasped.

Without doubt, he asserted, the jewelry was created by the Aztecs under Montezuma. He theorized that the gold bars had been molded and marked for the king of Spain. However, the archeologist said, there was no known report of a shipwreck in the colonial era from which such an astonishing treasure could have come. "This," he added, "is the most sensational hoard uncovered to date."

As word of the discovery spread up and down the Pacific Coast, treasure hunters from far and wide filled the surf, climbed every rock, and cruised in small boats close to land from the outskirts of Veracruz all the way to the ancient fortress of San Juan Ulua four miles to the north. The Mexican navy sent ships to patrol and to fend off illegal treasure hunters, and the Mexican army sent men to line the shores.

The Mexican government dispatched its own treasure hunters to the scene, determined to turn every grain of sand on the possibility that the Hurtado discovery represented only a portion of the total to be found.

How had the treasure gotten there? How much remained? The questions, the possibilities, excited the imagination. Clearly, the Hurtado find was captured gold, since much of it was stamped in the Spanish manner. But then why had it not found its way to a ship? Was the Hurtado bonanza merely the spillings from one small boat that had miscalculated the surf on a trip out to a galleon in the long loading process? Or a small cache that had been diverted from joining the main cargo by some unscrupulous sailor or colonial official?

After a period of intense but fruitless searching, government frogmen suspended their search, daunted by rough seas, clouded water, and especially the alarming quantity of sharks. A navy captain observed, "Nobody in his right mind would go into the water this time of year, not even for treasure."

Released on bail in time for Christmas while awaiting his trial, the jeweler Ortega miserably pronounced himself a ruined man. Hurtado, spending the last of his pesos on his own bail bond, became a poor octopus fisherman once again, braving the waters that had been too much for his country's professional divers. It was not that he wanted to, now; it was certainly not for treasure. It was, rather, for something to eat.

8. Adding It All Up

"I dread it when some of our friends visit," said the attractive young mother. She had no reason to be ashamed of her home. None at all. She and her husband, in their twenties, had become suddenly rich and bought a stately, wooded mansion. A highly recommended decorator had "done" their living room for $30,000. They liked it but sometimes were uncomfortable with its opulence.

"My son belongs to a play group," the woman said, "and I enjoy visiting the other mothers; they live in comfortable middle-class homes. But when it's their turn to come here, they feel uncomfortable, and so do I. There's whispering. I get uptight and feel very guilty," she said. "It's the same with some of our old friends, too. And it's hard to make new friends our age, because most people our age are struggling, and we have so much money."

One thing becomes overwhelmingly clear from listening to and hearing about the people who share the "suddenly rich

179

experience": The search for happiness does not necessarily
end when riches come, but the search for happiness almost
invariably, and of necessity, goes on. Judy Lutes, the Chicago
lottery winner, could finally treat herself to all the steaks she
wanted, but her life changed little otherwise; Barbara Ayash
escaped her "Rags" image with designer clothes, but found
that even multimillionaires can go broke; and cop Joe Wambaugh wrote himself out of a job he loved.

Money doesn't all by itself confer any special magic to
sweep away all problems, dissolve personality flaws, sweeten
human relationships, or deliver every heart's desire.

"Money can give you a lot, but you can't base your entire
happiness on it," said the psychoanalyst Dr. Gilberg. "With
whatever you get, you give up something, and that's part of
the human condition, which presents a continuing struggle to
maintain our balance. At best we can always be working for
perfection, but it's never going to be, and it takes a very ma-
ture individual to cope with that."

When sudden money comes into one's life and one sees
that it doesn't solve all his problems, it often intensifies one's
anxieties, Dr. Gilberg noted. "Some people have trouble
whether they're rich or poor, and some have no difficulty at all
under either condition. The issue is the individual." He believes that the people who deal best with the problems money
brings are the same people who would have dealt best with
their lives even if money had never come in abundance; this
seems a valid conclusion to be drawn from the stories presented.

"We were happy before, and we're happy now," said Ed
Henry, the down-to-earth New Jersey lottery millionaire. In
at least two other cases, the heiress Jolene Gearin and Barbara
Ayash, who married a millionaire, they came to realize that
money was not fulfilling their lives, and, indeed, only when
they lost their money did they "find themselves."

Those of the newly rich who run into troubles can't be
considered abnormal people. They experience a kind of

economic jet lag from what sociologists call "rapid status modification."

"Since money is correlated with one's status in society,
the impact of sudden wealth can be very traumatic," commented Dr. Lewis Yablonsky, a sociologist at California State
University. "You go into free fall—or perhaps free rise. All
your norms disappear. Your old values are no longer valid,
and this can be both exhilarating and frightening." Dr. Yablonsky, who lectures on how money influences people's lives,
has written several books on social problems and their treatment, including *The Tunnel Back* (Macmillan, 1965). He said:
"From a social point of view, most people have considerable
difficulty with rapid status modification. A sudden rise in
status—through money—can be very disorienting—
alienating."

Mobility takes a downward path, too, he reminded, also
with traumatic results which have been chronicled in the past.
"A sudden plunge in economic status, such as what happened
in 1929 when the fortunes of rich people suddenly
plummeted—well, we saw what happened. At least in a sudden climb in status, the psychic pain is soothed to a degree by
the benefits of wealth."

Social climbing seemed to take on a whole new perspec-
tive recently when that attractive young Pennsylvania couple
we met in the introduction, Tom and Philomena Drake, announced to the press that they had decided to sell everything
they owned and invest the money in lottery tickets for a crack
at the state's million-dollar top prize. Sensible people all over
the country shook their heads at the madness of it. "As
gamblers, they have a lot to learn," was the typical comment.
Syndicated columnist Tom Pierce put the odds against their
winning at about 35 million to one and added, "Even if the
Drakes should beat the odds, does happiness await them?"

Reacting to a news item about the couple, Dr. Roderic
Gorney, a psychiatrist with the School of Medicine at the University of California, Los Angeles, assailed the parental pose

struck by government in stimulating childish, unrealistic hopes through mass lotteries. He wrote in a letter appearing in the *Los Angeles Times*, "If what we want is a sturdy and independent populace, our elected representatives and public institutions ought to worry less about getting unfortunate people off welfare and more about not enticing them to remain infantile."

The better part of a year passed and the Drakes proceeded to sell their property and to empty their savings account, raising slightly more than $14,000, which they spent entirely on lottery tickets. Thousands of tickets passed through their hands, which the couple bought in batches worth hundreds of dollars, or $1,000, whatever money was on hand. In one final plunge they sank the last of their assets into a spree of 10,000 tickets, which they peeled and perused in public, exposing the unlucky numbers until Mrs. Drake's excitement turned to worry. But her husband urged her on with the thought that the next one could be The One.

When thousands of dollars' worth of the lottery tickets had been heaped in a trash pile with only a few of them scoring small payoffs of five dollars or less, tension set in, but before long the Drakes defied the odds by hitting a $10,000 prize. Dozens of smaller prizes followed, and when it was all added up, they found they had won more than $15,000, which not only repaid their entire original investment but gave them a bonus of a thousand dollars, plus 1,200 chances in an upcoming semifinal drawing that could advance them to the final stage and a shot at their real goal, the "instant millionaire" prize.

At the public semifinal drawing the Drakes were the stars, standing by in front of network television cameras and a phalanx of newsmen while the hundred finalists were selected one by one from a roller drum. The Drakes had so many tickets in that drum that they had reduced the odds significantly, from the original chance of more than a million to one all the way down to a mere 34 to one. When the last of the hundred names was drawn, the Drakes were not among them. Even at the lowered odds, the bet they had made was the same as if they had entered a casino and put all their chips on a number for one turn of the roulette wheel. Except that they had nothing to lose, money-wise, at that point.

Hesitating to begin all over again and reinvest their $15,000 in new batches of lottery tickets, the Drakes also rejected the observations of cautious people who pointed out that they might have gained as much profit by putting the money in a bank. Tom Drake, who still earned money in real estate, figured he had reaped a publicity bonus that was good for business, and he told the press that he'd been offered money to write about his experiences.

Whether or not they won isn't the point, beyond the horrible example it might have set, even though Drake took several opportunities to state publicly that other people should not copy their gamble. He told people he and his wife had no obligations, no children, and if nothing came of the enterprise they'd just go back to work. Had they won, their status as folk heroes would have been assured, for the Drakes' quest had captured the imagination of the public as strikingly as that of a tightrope walker or an endurance pilot. They were would-be economic Lindberghs. Their daring was something to which everyone could relate.

"The ideology of upward mobility is so firmly insinuated into our moral fibre that most people cannot perceive that there is anything wrong with it at all," wrote one sociologist, William Bruce Cameron, in *Informal Sociology* (Random House, 1963). "Anyone who needs money is vulnerable, and this means almost all of us in present-day society. The fact that we can so easily be convinced that we need just a little bit more is the real hobgoblin."

A Mexican fisherman and his entire family reveled in wealth on the equivalent of $5,000, but the Drakes, who had three times that much, felt so discontent that they were willing to risk it all on a chance for more. People in most parts of the world would puzzle over the curious behavior of the Drakes, and even a Depression-era American would have trouble un-

derstanding why a nice young couple with $15,000 would risk
every cent of it in a wild gamble with a goal of financial security!

Obviously, excitement is a factor, which is why many
people gamble. "Our national government," complained
James T. Adams in *The Tempo of Modern Life* (1931), "under-
took to inflame our American love of gambling and our desire to 'get rich quick' regardless of the effect on character."
That comment was written in the 1920's before the stock
market crash, so the Drakes' quest can't be regarded as something new in the American spirit.

It was a simple, clear-cut matter to Drake, as he told the
Associated Press: "When we win the million, we'll do what we
want for the rest of our lives."

Actually, he'd said little, because except for the money,
they already had the right to do that. As for the lottery, the
odds still are greater that they will inherit a fortune from a
stranger, strike oil in their back yard, or, given the same investment, gain sudden riches in dozens of other ways.

As statistical citizens, the odds were greater that
Philomena would get pregnant and have quadruplets, that
one of them would be in an automobile accident within the
year, or even that one of them would contract Legionaire's
Disease, than that they would become lottery millionaires.
The chances, good and bad, are out there for everyone to
face, and some measure of joy might be taken in the fact that
there are good things to balance out the bad. If the Drakes
were able to feel for a brief interval that they were guiding
their own destinies, the odds say this was an illusion.

One of the questions asked by columnists about the
Drakes was, "Even if they won, would happiness await them?"

Professor Philip Brickman of Northwestern University,
a social psychologist, conducted an interesting survey that at-
tempted to establish the relative happiness of lottery winners
in an unusual approach that compared the best of good fortune and the worst of misfortune, posing the same questions

to Illinois lottery winners and a like number of accident victims who had been paralyzed.

Brickman, assisted by graduate student Dan Coates and assistant professor Ronnie Janass Bulman of the University of Massachusetts, quizzed the lottery winners, accident victims, and a "control group" of similar persons who played the lottery but had never won, who drove the highways but had never crashed. The questions probed their general feelings of happiness as well as their level of enjoyment of various everyday pleasures such as talking with friends, eating a good meal, or reading. The outcome of the study indicated that happiness seems to depend not so much on the major good and bad strokes of fortune that happen to people—lottery luck or disability—but more on how these events compare with past experience. Incidentally, in the Brickman survey, both groups, accident victims and lottery winners, responded to the question, "Why me?" mostly with the answer, "God had a reason."

Such feelings, mentioned earlier in this book, may be less a religious testimonial than an additional support for the value people place on individual effort. People do not want to accept the idea that their lives can be directed by arbitrary, random happenings, so they attribute these mysteries to deity.

"An arbitrary world is threatening because it implies that one cannot control his rewards and punishments by means of his own actions," noted an article entitled "Belief in a Just World," in *The Journal of Social Issues.* "All of us need to believe that we live in a world in which we and others can get what we deserve," said the report from the Department of Social Relations at Harvard University. "As a result, we tend to believe that even ostensibly random rewards and punishments must in fact reflect an underlying moral order." That finding also was based on lottery surveys (through questioning the winners and losers in the Selective Service System's Vietnam draft lottery about their attitudes toward justice in the world) and does not contend that the Blind Lady can't see, but rather that we live by some curious concepts.

From sea to shining sea, from classroom to the unisex shop, we hallow the concept of equality, within the national borders, of course, and then we spend our days fighting the paradox of equality by trying to rise above our neighbors in the Status Wars. The better home, the new automobile, the luxurious restaurants we desire, may fit into categories of needs—shelter, transportation, food—but whether or not we believe suggestions that they will improve our sex lives, guarantee domestic harmony, and better fuel the body and spirit, we also use them as the status symbols they are, as marks of achievement, of the upwardly mobile who are a little bit better than their former equals.

Social comparison, whether it's gossip about how much an acquaintance spends for clothing, the salary of a sports star, or the faded tradition of keeping up with the Joneses, spans the gamut of our economic lives as we all struggle to become richer—if only richer than yesterday. "It isn't enough to succeed," the witty Gore Vidal once quipped, "one must also have a friend who fails."

Who wants equality if he can be rich instead?

"The higher classes in our society are better fed, better housed, better educated and live longer than their less fortunate fellow citizens," wrote Peter L. Berger, sociology professor and author of *The Precarious Vision* (Doubleday, 1961), adding, "There is a statistical correlation between the quantity of money one earns per annum and the number of years one may expect to do so on this earth."

One overweight lottery millionaire, puffing to the stage in his moment of glory, immediately grasped the concept of his prize, $50,000 a year for life, blurting out, "I'm going to lose weight and live a long time."

What people do with the money they have longed for as a natural goal of upward mobility reveals a great deal about the real goals behind our grander dreams. While a few prove themselves equal to the challenge of acting out their fantasies to the hilt, the majority of suddenly rich people we have met settled for buying new homes and new cars—the traditional rather than imaginative desires.

Those who squandered on the stuff of dreams sometimes seemed determined to throw away their fortunes. Happiest of the newly wealthy in many cases were those who stayed closest to their former lives or did not allow their money to derail prior goals, improving rather than transforming their lives and managing to cling to old friends. That may be encouraging to people of limited dreams, because a little money, not necessarily a lot, can be within their grasp and can make rich improvements. We may seek streets paved with gold, but most of us will settle for a nice house in a good neighborhood with the family and friends we already have.

Financial security itself seemed to be the major blessing for which most of the suddenly rich were thankful—in itself a limited dream, and something that should not be so rare among hard-working people. In fact, it constitutes a national economic shame that financial insecurity, which in most instances is really more a fear than a reality, should be so widespread that relief from it is the major dream fulfilled by those elevated from the ranks. The goal of The American Dream supposedly is "The Good Life," which should be available to more people through their efforts rather than chance. Otherwise, the odds against reaching the destination of upward mobility mean most of us may be wasting our lives while waiting to live. If financial insecurity can only be relieved through such windfall dreams as lottery prizes, maybe we'd better learn to live with it and make the best of the pleasures and limited leisure at hand.

It seems evident that even to those windfall heroes whose new wealth primarily meant freedom from having to work for a living, the problem of time on their hands emerged. Apparently, few of us are prepared for leisure.

We are a hard-working people whose respect for labor—not always justified—stems from religious roots, government, and even our parents. In a 1977 survey on American values conducted by General Mills, an amazing 96 percent of parents listed foremost among the values they want to pass along to their children the belief that the only way to get ahead in life is hard work. Even more amazing perhaps, a third of these parents weren't sure they still believed in this work ethic themselves. Where had it gotten them?

Studs Terkel, in his sometimes terrifying, sometimes inspiring book *Working* (Random House, 1974) suggested that the time has come for revising the work ethic. Even psychiatry is taking a new look at man's need for work. Wrote psychoanalyst Gilberg in a paper addressed to his colleagues, "Freud, we know, felt that one sign of healthy life was work." However, Gilberg pointed out, the changing society today encourages or recognizes the choices of other lifestyles, sometimes subsidized officially through welfare. Gilberg noted, "The concept of work as we know it, and even as we work, needs review."

To the vast majority of Americans the concept of work stands in such undisputed respect that they join the wealthy in boasting about how many long hours they put in even though they prosper little. We pursue leisure with a sort of guilt at its idleness, and it's no wonder that leisure has a bad reputation and little interest as a vocation: except in the cases of old age and unemployment—both usually involving a demeaning shortage of funds—we have little favorable experience with it.

Perhaps we need a new concept of leisure, too, something that doesn't carry the connotation of loitering or malingering or waste. If labor has dignity and leisure is its goal, we should have a dignity of leisure.

Some sociologists see dire significance in the fact that many of those who become financially able to quit their jobs do so, but there should have been many more who quit if leisure is accepted as a true goal of upward mobility—the situation in which people are able, as the Drakes wanted, "to do anything we want the rest of our lives."

Many of the suddenly rich who quit work do so because the Internal Revenue Service makes it almost a total loss for people with other income to work for a paycheck. Nobody can be motivated to work for nothing, but payment can be in either satisfaction or money. When a job means nothing more than a hard-earned paycheck, people are eager to leave. Still, many of the newly rich do continue working, even when their jobs carry little status or future—for example, factory workers or secretaries who need work as a social activity, lest too much leisure become a burden.

The Institute for Social Research has declared, "For most of the men in our culture, work is apparently the sole organizing principle and the only means of self-expression." Without work, they assert, men "exhibit a certain deterioration of personality, loss of emotional stability, breakdown of morale, new faults such as drinking, unfaithfulness, and so on." This description sounds as devastating as the aftermath of a drug or vice; but our findings disagree, at least when the idleness is voluntary and money is present, although some cases do follow a pattern of deterioration. Psychoanalysts and sociologists point out, and our stories support the conclusion, that men and women suffer equally when their lives lack a self-fulfilling pursuit or occupation, independent of whether they are rich or poor. But routine, tiresome jobs don't fill their needs. In fact, it's precisely from such work that millions want to flee.

If all Americans in the future find the greatly expanded leisure that sociologists expect, and that the burgeoning industry of fun and games anticipates, people had better start now pretending they are going to be rich soon and seek rewarding ways to spend their idle hours. "The problem of leisure today does not confront only the wealthy," observed Franz Alexander, adding, "The majority of the population will find itself more and more confronted with the problem of how to spend their free time." And he foretold the ravages of "malignant boredom, a disease which threatens not a specific organ of the body but the organism as a whole. It deprives man of the meaning of life and undermines his wish to live."

The introduction to this book pondered whether it is

advisable to move very far from our economic and social origins as the suddenly rich are free to do. As surely as the immigrants to America probed its western limits step by step to the farthest ocean, it is an inevitable economic and social journey, and perhaps it is not too prosaic to look upon those making it as explorers of a destination to which all aspire, bringing back reliable information on the dangers of the trip and the beauty of the terrain.

"What do you want? You want the moon?" For centuries men looked up to that golden satellite, and when transportation was available, the trip was made. They found desert-in-the-round, with terrific scenery but no other treasures worth the fare for ordinary tastes. In fact, it looked better from a distance—and more romantic.

If the exploration of the phenomenon of sudden riches has illustrated something of the same kind of report, perhaps the question about rising far from our economic origins is answered. Like the moon or the coast that always seemed so far, wealth can be beautiful and barren, exciting and placid, largely depending on what you bring with you. But at least we know the journey can be made—and not just by other-worldly creatures akin to Hughes or Rockefeller, but by ordinary people.

From these reports, some of us may decide that we don't want to make the trip quite so hurriedly or even as far as we thought—we may try to enjoy the trip rather than the destination—but others will be all the more eager.

To some extent it's sad that, for the vast majority of people, it's only through twists of fortune that they'll ever get there. But in the eyes of half of the world, the American, struggling though he may be in his own eyes, already is rich. As the pollster George Gallup told a Senate committee in 1977, reporting on a Global Survey on Human Needs and Satisfactions, more than half of the world is engaged in an unending struggle for the barest level of survival. "Only in the Western World," he said, "can the inhabitants engage in anything akin to a 'pursuit of happiness.' "

Thus prosperity and happiness are related situations, which agrees with our last major, if obvious, finding among all the questions posed and answered to varying degrees in this many-faceted exploration of the subject: Rich is better. Not just because everybody seems to want it. More convincingly, from all our contacts, no matter what problems money brought, not one of the suddenly rich wished it had never happened—or tried to give it back.